Greater Sage-grouse

(*Centrocercus urophasianus*)

Conservation Objectives: Final Report

February 2013

United States Department of the Interior

FISH AND WILDLIFE SERVICE
Washington, D.C. 20240
MAR 2 2 2013

Dear Interested Reader:

Last spring, I asked each state within the range of the greater sage-grouse to join the U.S. Fish and Wildlife Service (Service) in a first-of-its-kind, collaborative approach to develop range-wide conservation objectives for the sage-grouse, both to inform our upcoming 2015 decision under the Endangered Species Act and to inform the collective conservation efforts of the many partners working to conserve the species. Recognizing that state wildlife agencies have management expertise and management authority for sage-grouse, we convened a Conservation Objectives Team (COT) of state and Service representatives. I asked the team to produce a recommendation regarding the degree to which threats need to be reduced or ameliorated to conserve the greater sage-grouse so that it would no longer be in danger of extinction or likely to become in danger of extinction in the foreseeable future.

The final, peer-reviewed COT report (attached here) delineates such objectives, based upon the best scientific and commercial data available at the time of its release. I would like to clarify here the Service's interpretation of a few issues that I know are of interest to our state partners.

The highest level objective identified in the report is to minimize habitat threats to the species so as to meet the objective of the 2006 Western Association of Fish and Wildlife Agencies' (WAFWA) Greater Sage-grouse Comprehensive Conservation Strategy: reversing negative population trends and achieving a neutral or positive population trend. The Service interprets this recommendation to mean that actions and measures should be put in place now that will eventually arrest what has been a continuing declining trend. Conservation success will be achieved by removing or reducing threats to the species now, such that population trends will eventually be stable or increasing, even if numbers are not restored to historic levels. In addition, while the WAFWA Greater Sage-grouse Comprehensive Conservation Strategy overall objective is tied to ecologically delineated Management Zones for this species, the Service may measure conservation success by evaluating population trends at other appropriate scales.

One key component of this report is the identification of Priority Areas of Conservation (PACs), which were described as key habitats that are essential for sage-grouse conservation. PACs were identified using the best available information at the time of the team's completion of the report. The report acknowledges the uncertainties associated in the delineation of these areas, yet focuses our attention on these areas. These areas were identified as highly important for long term viability of the species and should be a primary focus of our collective conservation efforts. The team, however, expressed in the report that new information may come to light indicating that some areas outside the identified PACs are also highly important. This could be due to their significance for a critical life history phase, or as a link to ensure connectivity to other populations, or to retain opportunities for critical restoration efforts that may come to light in the future. If information comes to light indicating an area outside a PAC is highly important, state and federal partners working to conserve the species should consider its significance as decisions are made that could impact that area.

Therefore, the report encourages, but does not require, that important habitats outside of PACs be conserved to the extent possible. In addition, page 36 of the COT Report indicates that states with state plans developed in conjunction with the Service should follow those plans in making decisions about areas outside of PACs.

The report identifies conservation objectives and measures for each of the habitat threats assessed. For some threats, the team identified examples of actions that could be used to help attain the conservation objectives, and they termed these "conservation options." The Service interprets these "options" as suggestions and examples only, not prescriptive or mandatory actions. These options were provided by the team to stimulate discussions important in the development of conservation planning efforts that will achieve the conservation objectives in the report.

The development of this report reflects a truly collaborative federal-state effort designed to provide a clearer picture of objectives that, if met, will ensure the long-term, robust persistence of this iconic western species. Achieving these conservation objectives will require our continuing collaboration. The Service appreciates the dedication of our colleagues from the western states who joined with us to develop this report.

Sincerely,

DIRECTOR

Greater Sage-grouse

(Centrocercus urophasianus)

Conservation Objectives: Final Report

February 2013

PREFACE

This report delineates reasonable objectives, based upon the best scientific and commercial data available at the time of its release, for the conservation and survival of greater sage-grouse. Individual team members contributed by providing technical information and data, participating in critical discussions, providing critical reviews and edits, or authoring sections of the report. While the team tried to achieve consensus it was not always achieved. The report is provided to the Director, USFWS, at his request, to provide additional information for his use and consideration pertinent to future decision making relative to greater sage-grouse. The report will also serve as guidance to federal land management agencies, state sage-grouse teams, and others in focusing efforts to achieve effective conservation for this species.

Team members included:
- Bob Budd, State of Wyoming
- Dave Budeau, Oregon Department of Fish and Wildlife
- Dr. John Connelly, Idaho Department of Fish and Game
- Shawn Espinosa, Nevada Department of Wildlife
- Scott Gardner, California Department of Fish and Wildlife
- Dr. Kathy Griffin, Colorado Parks and Wildlife
- John Harja, State of Utah
- Rick Northrup, Montana Fish, Wildlife & Parks
- Aaron Robinson, North Dakota Game and Fish
- Dr. Michael Schroeder, Washington Department of Fish and Wildlife
- Steve Abele, U.S. Fish and Wildlife Service, Nevada
- Dr. Pat Deibert, U.S. Fish and Wildlife Service, Region 6
- Jodie Delavan, U.S. Fish & Wildlife Service, Oregon
- Paul Souza, U.S. Fish & Wildlife Service, Headquarters
- James Lindstrom, U.S. Fish & Wildlife Service, Wyoming (cartographer)

Assistance with review and editing of the document was provided by Jesse D'Elia (U.S. Fish and Wildlife Service). We also thank Don Kemner from the Idaho Department of Fish and Game for thoughtful comments.

This report is guidance only; identification of conservation objectives and measures does not create a legal obligation beyond existing legal requirements. Nothing in this plan should be construed as a commitment or requirement that any federal agency obligate or pay funds in contravention of the Anti-Deficiency Act, 31 U.S.C. 1341, or any other law or regulation. The objectives in this report are subject to modification as dictated by new findings, changes in species' status, and the completion of conservation actions.

RECOMMENDED CITATION

U.S. Fish and Wildlife Service. 2013. Greater Sage-grouse (*Centrocercus urophasianus*) Conservation Objectives: Final Report. U.S. Fish and Wildlife Service, Denver, CO. February 2013.

TABLE OF CONTENTS

LIST OF FIGURES

LIST OF TABLES

1.   BACKGROUND AND PURPOSE

On March 23, 2010, the U. S. Fish and Wildlife Service (FWS) determined that the greater sage-grouse (*Centrocercus urophasianus*; sage-grouse) warranted the protections of the Endangered Species Act of 1973, as amended, 1531 *et seq.* (ESA), but that adding it to the List of Endangered and Threatened Wildlife under the ESA was precluded by higher priority listing actions. Species found to be warranted for listing but precluded by higher priority listing actions ("warranted but precluded") are placed on the federal list of candidate species under the ESA.[1] Shortly after the sage-grouse became a candidate species, the FWS entered into a court-approved settlement agreement with several environmental groups which formalized a schedule for making listing determinations on over 200 candidate species nationwide, including the sage-grouse and its Distinct Population Segments (DPSs). The court-approved schedule indicates that a decision on whether to proceed with listing sage-grouse, or withdrawing our warranted finding, is due by September 2015.[2]

Given the broad implications of potentially listing the sage-grouse under the ESA, in December 2011, Wyoming Governor Matt Mead and Secretary of the Interior Ken Salazar co-hosted a meeting to address coordinated conservation of the sage-grouse across its range. Ten states within the range of the sage-grouse were represented[3], as were the U.S. Forest Service (FS), the Natural Resources Conservation Service (NRCS), and the Department of the Interior (DOI) — including representatives from the DOI's Bureau of Land Management (BLM) and U.S. Fish and Wildlife Service (FWS). The primary outcome of the meeting was the creation of a Sage-Grouse Task Force (Task Force) chaired by Governors Mead (WY) and Hickenlooper (CO) and the Director of the BLM. The Task Force was directed to develop recommendations on how to best advance a coordinated, multi-state, range-wide effort to conserve the sage-grouse, including the identification of conservation objectives to ensure the long-term viability of the species.

With the backing of the Task Force, the Director of FWS tasked staff with the development of range-wide conservation objectives for the sage-grouse to define the degree to which threats need to be reduced or ameliorated to conserve sage-grouse so that it is no longer in danger of extinction or likely to become in danger of extinction in the foreseeable future. Recognizing that state wildlife agencies have management expertise and management authority for sage-grouse, the FWS created a Conservation Objectives Team (COT) of state and FWS representatives (see Preface, above) to accomplish this task. Each member was selected by his or her state or agency. This report is the outcome of the COT's efforts.

---

[1] Two distinct population segments (DPSs) of sage-grouse are also on the candidate list – the Columbia Basin DPS (in Washington State) and the Bi-State population (in California and western Nevada).

[2] A decision on whether or not to proceed with listing the Bi-State population is due by September 2013. A decision on whether or not to proceed with listing the Columbia Basin DPS is due by September 2015.

[3] California, Colorado, Idaho, Montana, Nevada, Oregon, South Dakota, Utah, Washington, and Wyoming

2.   SAGE-GROUSE BIOLOGY AND CURRENT STATUS

The greater sage-grouse is the largest North American grouse species and one of only two sage-grouse species in the world; the other is the Gunnison sage-grouse (*Centrocercus minimus*).

Prior to European settlement in the 19th century, sage-grouse inhabited 13 western states and three Canadian provinces, and their potential habitat covered over 1.2 million square kilometers (km^2) (0.46 million square miles (mi^2); Schroeder *et al.* 2004). Sage-grouse have declined across their range due to a variety of causes and now occupy 56 percent of their historic range (Schroeder *et al.* 2004; Figure 1). They currently occur in 11 states and two Canadian provinces (Knick and Connelly 2011). The actual decline in the number of sage-grouse from pre-settlement times is unclear as estimates of greater sage-grouse abundance were mostly anecdotal prior to the implementation of systematic surveys in the 1950s (Braun 1998).

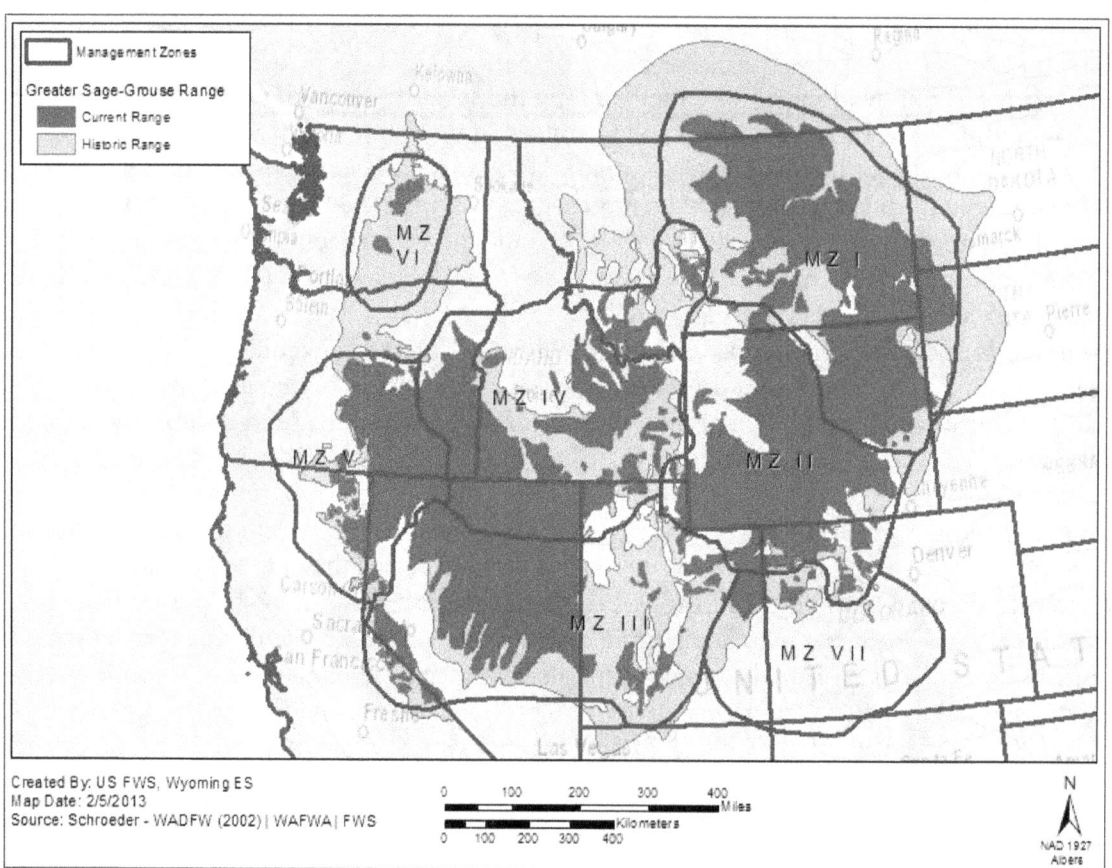

Figure 1. The current (occupied since the late 1990s) and historic (maximum distribution from the 1800s to early 1990s) range of the greater sage-grouse (Schroeder et al. 2004).

Sage-grouse depend on a variety of semiarid shrub-grassland (shrub steppe) habitats throughout their life cycle, and are considered obligate users of sagebrush (e.g., *Artemisia tridentata* ssp. *wyomingensis* (Wyoming big sagebrush), *A. t.* ssp. *vaseyana* (mountain big sagebrush), and *A. t. tridentata* (basin big sagebrush)) (Patterson 1952; Braun *et al.* 1976; Connelly *et al.* 2000;

Connelly *et al.* 2004; Miller *et al.* 2011). Sage-grouse also use other sagebrush species (which can be locally important) such as *A. arbuscula* (low sagebrush), *A. nova* (black sagebrush), *A. frigida* (fringed sagebrush), and *A. cana* (silver sagebrush) (Schroeder *et al.* 1999; Connelly *et al.* 2004). Sage-grouse distribution is strongly correlated with the distribution of sagebrush habitats (Schroeder *et al.* 2004; Connelly *et al.* 2011b). Sage-grouse exhibit strong site fidelity (loyalty to a particular area) to seasonal habitats (i.e., breeding, nesting, brood rearing, and wintering areas) (Connelly *et al.* 2004; Connelly *et al.* 2011a). Adult sage-grouse rarely switch from these habitats once they have been selected, limiting their ability to respond to changes in their local environments (Schroeder *et al.* 1999).

During the breeding season, in spring, male sage-grouse gather together to perform courtship displays on areas called leks. Leks are typically relatively bare areas, where males perform courtship displays to attract females, surrounded by a sagebrush-grassland, which is used for escape cover, nesting, and foraging. The proximity, configuration, and abundance of nesting habitat are key factors influencing lek locations (Connelly *et al.* 1981, Connelly *et al.* 2011a).

Productive nesting areas are typically characterized by sagebrush with an understory of native grasses and forbs, with horizontal and vertical structural diversity that provides an insect prey base, herbaceous forage for pre-laying and nesting hens, and cover for the hen while she is incubating (Gregg 1991; Schroeder *et al.* 1999; Connelly *et al.* 2000; Connelly *et al.* 2004; Connelly *et al.* 2011b). Shrub canopy and grass cover provide concealment for sage-grouse nests and young and are critical for reproductive success (Barnett and Crawford 1994; Gregg *et al.* 1994; DeLong *et al.* 1995; Connelly *et al.* 2004). Because average clutch sizes is 7 eggs (Connelly *et al.* 2011a), and sage-grouse exhibit limited re-nesting, there is little evidence that populations of sage-grouse produce large annual surpluses (Connelly *et al.* 2011a).

Most sage-grouse gradually move from sagebrush uplands to more mesic areas (moist areas, such as streambeds or wet meadows) during the late brood-rearing period (three weeks post-hatch) in response to summer desiccation of herbaceous vegetation in the sagebrush uplands (Connelly *et al.* 2000). Summer use areas can include sagebrush habitats as well as riparian areas, wet meadows and alfalfa fields (Schroeder *et al.* 1999). These areas provide an abundance of forbs and insects for both hens and chicks (Schroeder *et al.* 1999; Connelly *et al.* 2000). This is important because forbs and insects are essential nutritional components for chicks (Klebenow and Gray 1968; Johnson and Boyce 1991; Connelly *et al.* 2004; Thompson *et al.* 2006). Late brood-rearing habitats are often associated with sagebrush, but selection is based on the availability of forbs, correlating with a shift in the diet of chicks as they mature (Connelly *et al.* 1988, and references therein; Connelly *et al.* 2011b). As vegetation continues to desiccate through the late summer and fall, sage-grouse shift their diet entirely to sagebrush (Schroeder *et al.* 1999) and depend entirely on sagebrush throughout the winter for both food and cover (Schroeder *et al.* 1999).

Many sage-grouse move between seasonal ranges in response to habitat distribution (Connelly *et al.* 2004; Fedy *et al.* 2012). Movement can occur between winter, breeding, and summer areas; between breeding, summer and winter areas; or, not at all. Movement distances of up to 161 km (100 mi) have been recorded (Patterson 1952; Tack *et al.* 2011; Smith 2013); however, distances vary depending on the locations of seasonal habitats (Schroeder *et al.* 1999). Information regarding the distribution and characteristics of movement corridors for sage-grouse is very limited (Connelly *et al.* 2004); although, in a few areas monitoring of radio-collared birds has provided some insights into seasonal movement patterns (e.g., Smith 2013). These movement corridors are considered "traditional", as birds do not always select the most proximal habitats (Connelly *et al.* 1988; Connelly *et al.* 2011a). Sage-grouse dispersal (permanent moves to other areas) is poorly understood (Connelly *et al.* 2004) and appears to be sporadic (Dunn and Braun 1986).

Sage-grouse are dependent on large areas of contiguous sagebrush (Patterson 1952; Connelly *et al.* 2004; Connelly *et al.* 2011a; Wisdom *et al.* 2011). Large-scale disturbances (e.g., agricultural conversions) within surrounding landscapes influence sage-grouse habitat selection (Knick and Hanser 2011) and population persistence (Aldridge *et al.* 2008; Wisdom *et al.* 2011). Sagebrush is the most widespread vegetation in the intermountain lowlands of the western United States (West and Young 2000); however, sagebrush is considered one of the most imperiled ecosystems in North America due to continued degradation and lack of protection (Knick *et al.* 2003; Miller *et al.* 2011, and references therein). Not all sagebrush provides suitable habitat for sage-grouse due to fragmentation and degradation (Schroeder *et al.* 2004). Sage-grouse avoid areas where humans have caused sagebrush fragmentation, but not naturally fragmented landscapes (Leu and Hanser 2011). Very little extant sagebrush is undisturbed, with up to 50 to 60 percent having altered understories or having been lost to direct conversions (Knick *et al.* 2003).

Sagebrush is long-lived, with plants of some species surviving at least 150 years (West 1983). Sagebrush has resistance to environmental extremes, with the exception of fire and occasionally defoliating insects (e.g., webworm (*Aroga* spp.); West 1983). Most species of sagebrush are killed by fire (West 1983; Miller and Eddleman 2000; West and Young 2000), and historic fire-return intervals have been as long as 350 years, depending on sagebrush type and environmental conditions (Baker 2011). Natural sagebrush re-colonization in burned areas depends on the presence of adjacent live plants for a seed source or on the seed bank (Miller and Eddleman 2000), and requires decades for full recovery. Due to its low intrinsic resistance to fire and long recovery times, the sagebrush ecosystem is particularly susceptible to increases in fire return intervals.

There is little information available regarding minimum sagebrush patch size required to support populations of sage-grouse. This is due in part to the migratory nature of some, but not all sage-grouse populations; the lack of proximal seasonal habitats; and differences in local, regional and range-wide ecological conditions that influence the distribution of sagebrush and its associated understory. Where home ranges have been reported (Connelly *et al.* 2011a and references therein), they are extremely variable (4 to 615 km^2 (1.5 to 237.5 mi^2)). Home range occupancy is related to multiple variables associated with both local vegetation characteristics and landscape characteristics (Knick *et al.* 2003; Leu and Hanser 2011). Pyke (2011) estimated that greater than 4,000 ha (9,884 ac) was necessary for population sustainability; however, Pyke did not indicate whether this value considered groups of birds that moved long distances between seasonal habitats versus those who can meet all necessary seasonal requirements within a local area, nor if this included juxtaposition of all seasonal habitats. Large seasonal and annual movements emphasize the need for large, functional landscapes to support viable sage-grouse populations (Knick *et al.* 2003; Connelly *et al.* 2011a).

3. SUMMARY OF THREATS

The following is a brief overview of the threats to sage-grouse and sagebrush habitats. For a more complete discussion, the reader is referred to the FWS 2010 warranted but precluded finding for this species (75 FR 13910).

The loss and fragmentation of sagebrush habitats is a primary cause of the decline of sage-grouse populations (Patterson 1952; Connelly and Braun 1997; Braun 1998; Johnson and Braun 1999; Connelly *et al.* 2000; Miller and Eddleman 2000; Schroeder and Baydack 2001; Johnsgard 2002; Aldridge and Brigham 2003; Beck *et al.* 2003; Pedersen *et al.* 2003; Connelly *et al.* 2004; Schroeder *et al.* 2004; Leu and Hanser 2011; 75 FR 13910). Habitat fragmentation, largely a result of human activities, can result in reductions in lek persistence, lek attendance, population recruitment, yearling and adult annual survival, female nest site selection, nest initiation, and complete loss of leks and winter habitat (Holloran 2005; Aldridge and Boyce 2007; Walker *et al.* 2007; Doherty *et al.* 2008). Functional habitat loss also contributes to habitat fragmentation, as greater sage-grouse avoid areas due to human activities, including noise, even though sagebrush remains intact (Blickley *et al.* 2012). In an analysis of population connectivity, Knick and Hanser (2011) demonstrated that in some areas of the sage-grouse's range, populations are already isolated and at risk for extirpation due to genetic, demographic, and stochastic (i.e., unpredictable) events such as lightning caused wildfire. Habitat loss and fragmentation contribute to the population's isolation and increased risk of extirpation.

Very little sagebrush within the range of the sage-grouse remains undisturbed or unaltered from its condition prior to Euro American settlement in the 1800s (Knick *et al.* 2003, and references therein). Disturbed or altered habitats have less resilience than intact habitats. Due to the disruption of primary patterns, processes and components of sagebrush ecosystems since Euro American settlement (Knick *et al.* 2003; Miller *et al.* 2011), the large range of abiotic variation, the minimal short-lived seed banks, and the long generation time of sagebrush, restoration of disturbed areas is very difficult. Not all areas previously dominated by sagebrush can be restored because alteration of vegetation, nutrient cycles, topsoil, and living (cryptobiotic) soil crusts has exceeded recovery thresholds (Knick *et al.* 2003; Pyke 2011). Additionally, processes to restore healthy native sagebrush communities are relatively unknown (Knick *et al.* 2003). Active restoration activities are often limited by financial and logistic resources (Knick *et al.* 2003; Miller *et al.* 2011) and may require decades or centuries (Knick *et al.* 2003, and references therein). Landscape restoration efforts require a broad range of partnerships (private, state, and federal) due to landownership patterns (Knick *et al.* 2003). Except for areas where active restoration is attempted following disturbance (e.g., mining, wildfire), management efforts in sagebrush ecosystems are usually focused on maintaining the remaining sagebrush (Miller *et al.* 2011; Wisdom *et al.* 2011).

Fire is one of the primary factors linked to loss of sagebrush-steppe habitat and corresponding population declines of greater sage-grouse (Connelly and Braun 1997; Miller and Eddleman 2001). Loss of sagebrush habitat to wildfire has been increasing in the western portion of the greater sage-grouse range due to an increase in fire frequency. The increase in mean fire frequency in sagebrush ecosystems has been facilitated by the incursion of nonnative annual grasses, primarily *Bromus tectorum* (cheatgrass) and *Taeniatherum asperum* (medusahead) (Billings 1994; Miller and Eddleman 2001). The positive feedback loop between exotic annual grasses and fires can preclude the opportunity for sagebrush to become re-established. Exotic annual grasses and other invasive plants also alter habitat suitability for sage-grouse by reducing or eliminating native forbs and grasses essential for food and cover. Annual grasses and noxious perennials continue to expand their range, facilitated by ground disturbances, including wildfire (Miller and Eddleman 2001; Balch *et al.* 2013), improper grazing (Young *et al.* 1972, 1976), agriculture (Benvenuti 2007), and infrastructure associated with energy development (Bergquist *et al.* 2007). Concern with habitat loss and fragmentation due to fire and invasive plants has mostly been focused in the western portion of the species' range. However, climate change may alter the range of invasive plants, potentially expanding the importance of this threat into other areas of the species' range.

Habitat loss is occurring from the expansion of native conifers (e.g., pinyon-pine (*Pinus edulis*) and juniper (*Juniperus* spp.) [pinyon-juniper]), mainly due to changes in fire return intervals and the overstocking of domestic livestock, particularly during the latter 1800's and early 1900's (Miller and Rose 1999); however, these factors may not entirely explain the expansion of western juniper (Soulé and Knapp 1999). Conifer encroachment may be facilitated by increases in global carbon dioxide (CO_2) concentrations, and climate change, but the influence of CO_2 has not been supported by some research (Archer *et al.* 1995).

Sage-grouse populations can be significantly reduced, and in some cases locally extirpated, by non-renewable energy development activities, even when mitigative measures are implemented (Walker *et al.* 2007). The persistent and increasing demand for energy resources is resulting in their continued development within sage-grouse range, and may cause further habitat fragmentation. Although data are limited, impacts resulting from renewable energy development are expected to have negative effects to sage-grouse populations and habitats due to their similarity in supporting infrastructure (Becker *et al.* 2009; Hagen 2010; LeBeau 2012; USFWS 2012). Both non-renewable and renewable energy developments are increasing within the range of sage-grouse, and this growth is likely to continue given current and projected demands for energy.

Other factors associated with habitat loss and fragmentation are summarized by Knick *et al.* (2011) and include conversion of sagebrush habitats for agriculture, the expanding human populations in the western United States and the resulting urban development in sagebrush habitats, vegetation treatments resulting in the alteration or removal of sagebrush to enhance grazing for livestock, and impacts from wild ungulates and free-roaming equids (horses and burros).

Other threats that can negatively affect sage-grouse include, but are not limited to, parasites, infectious diseases, predation, and weather events (e.g., drought or late spring storms). Some of these threats may be localized and of short duration, but may be significant at the local population and habitat level, particularly for small populations. An example of this local effect was the 2008 outbreak of West Nile virus (WNv) in the sage-grouse population of southwestern North Dakota. Having no resistance to this threat (Walker and Naugle 2011), sage-grouse population numbers in North Dakota dropped dramatically following the WNv outbreak. Four years later (2012), the population had improved but not fully recovered to levels seen before the outbreak (North Dakota Game and Fish Department, unpublished data).

Predation is often identified as a potential factor affecting sage-grouse populations, which is understandable given the suite of predators that prey on sage-grouse from egg to adulthood (though no predators specialize on sage-grouse). Predator management has been effective on local scales for short periods, but its efficacy over broad ranges or over long timespans has not been demonstrated (Hagen 2011a). In areas of compromised habitats and high populations of synanthropic predators (predators that live near, and benefit from, an association with humans), predator control may be effective to ensure sage-grouse persistence until habitat conditions improve.

Though threats such as infectious diseases and predation may be significant at a localized level, particularly if habitat quantity and quality is compromised, they were not identified by FWS as significant range-wide threats in our 2010 warranted finding (75 FR 13910).

The occurrence and importance of each of the above threats to sage-grouse varies across the species' range. For example, fire and invasive weeds are the primary issue in the western portion of the species' range, while non-renewable energy development affects primarily the eastern portion of the species' range (75 FR 13910). However, no part of the species' range is immune from any of the primary threats described above. Additionally, the impact of threats on local sage-grouse populations likely varies based on the resilience of that population and its associated habitats. Healthy, robust sagebrush and seasonal habitats and associated sage-grouse populations with few or no other threats are likely to be more resilient than habitats already experiencing a high level of threats, or in poor condition. Natural conditions, such as long-term drought, can also affect habitat and population resilience. To capture the variability in threats and population resilience across the range of the sage-grouse we assessed threats to each population (see section 4, below).

The lack of sufficient regulatory mechanisms to conserve sage-grouse and their habitats was identified as a primary threat leading to our warranted but precluded finding in 2010 (75 FR 13910). While specific regulatory mechanisms are not addressed in this report, federal land management agencies, and many state and local governments across the species' range are working to develop adequate mechanisms to address this threat. For example, Wyoming's Governor Dave Freudenthal was among the first to enact regulatory mechanisms to protect core sage-grouse areas through Executive Order 2010-4. Governor Matt Mead signed an updated version of the Sage-Grouse Core Area Protection Executive Order in 2011 (Executive Order 2011-5). The Wyoming Executive Orders apply to all regulatory actions governed by the State of Wyoming, and as such, constitute substantial regulatory mechanisms that contribute to the conservation of sage-grouse. These efforts demonstrate the potential for successfully ameliorating the primary threats to sage-grouse and their habitat through the development and implementation of sufficient regulatory mechanisms.

4. CONSERVATION FRAMEWORK

Our conservation framework consisted of (1) identifying sage-grouse population and habitat status and threats (**see Section 2 and 3**, above), (2) defining a broad conservation goal (see **Section 4.2 section**, below), (3) identifying priority areas for conservation (see **this section**, below), and (4) developing specific conservation objectives and measures (see **Section 4.3**, below). We used three parameters—population and habitat representation, redundancy, and resilience (Shaffer and Stein 2010, Redford *et al.* 2011)—as guiding concepts in developing our conservation goal, priority areas for conservation, conservation objectives, and measures.

4.1 Guiding Concepts – Redundancy, Representation, and Resilience

Redundancy is defined as multiple, geographically dispersed populations and habitats across a species' range, such that the loss of one population or one unit of habitat will not result in the loss of the species. Redundancy allows for a margin of safety for a species and/or its habitat to withstand threats, including unforeseen catastrophes.

Representation is defined as the retention of genetic, morphological, physiological, behavioral, habitat, or ecological diversity of the species so its adaptive capabilities are conserved.

Resilience is defined as the ability of the species and/or its habitat to recover from disturbances. In general species are likely to be more resilient if large populations exist in large blocks of high quality habitat across the full breadth of environmental variability to which the species is adapted (Redford *et al.* 2011).

Redundancy, representation, and resilience were examined with respect to sage-grouse populations and their habitat. Populations are defined as a group of individuals occupying an area of sufficient size to permit normal dispersal and/or migration behavior in which numerical changes are largely determined by birth and death processes (Berryman 2002). Sage-grouse populations followed those identified in Garton *et al.* (2011), with the exception of Utah where populations were refined based on local population data provided by the State of Utah.

For sage-grouse, retaining redundancy, representation, and resilience means having multiple and geographically distributed sage-grouse populations across the species' ecological niche and geographic range. Large populations distributed across large areas are generally less vulnerable to extinction than small populations (Soulé 1987, Shaffer and Stein 2010). By conserving well distributed sage-grouse populations across geographic and ecological gradients, species adaptive traits can be preserved, and populations can be maintained at levels that make sage-grouse more resilient in the face of catastrophes or environmental change.

4.2   Conservation Goal

We defined our conservation goal as the long-term conservation of sage-grouse and healthy sagebrush shrub and native perennial grass and forb communities by maintaining viable, connected, and well-distributed populations and habitats across their range, through threat amelioration, conservation of key habitats, and restoration activities.

4.3   Priority Areas for Conservation

Effective conservation strategies are predicated on identifying key areas across the landscape that are necessary to maintain redundant, representative, and resilient populations. Fortunately, most of the individual states within the range of sage-grouse have already undertaken considerable efforts to identify and map key habitats necessary for sage-grouse conservation in the development of their state management plans for this species. We used these existing maps to identify the most important areas needed for maintaining sage-grouse representation, redundancy, and resilience across the landscape. These areas were named *Priority Areas for Conservation* (PACs) (Figure 2).

Although different techniques and processes were used across states to identify PACs, all used relatively similar population- and habitat-based data sources (Table 1).

Where PACs did not match at state boundaries efforts were made to resolve discrepancies. Most of the discrepancies were the result of mapping errors that were subsequently resolved, management differences that followed state boundaries due to differing regulatory mechanisms, or land ownership patterns between two states. Unresolved boundary concerns are being actively addressed by the states and PAC boundaries will be amended as these discrepancies are resolved.

There is substantial overlap between our PAC map and the preliminary priority habitat maps BLM developed for their range-wide Resource Management Plan revisions. This is because both efforts used maps provided by the states. The primary differences are in Nevada and Utah, where the map developed by these states does not exactly match the preliminary BLM planning map. Where there were unresolved differences, we used state maps to identify PACs, as states have the most complete local information of sage-grouse distribution and habitat use.

PACs do not represent individual populations, but rather key areas that states have identified as crucial to ensure adequate representation, redundancy, and resilience for conservation of its associated population or populations. Additional finer scale planning efforts by states may determine that additional areas outside of PACs are also essential.

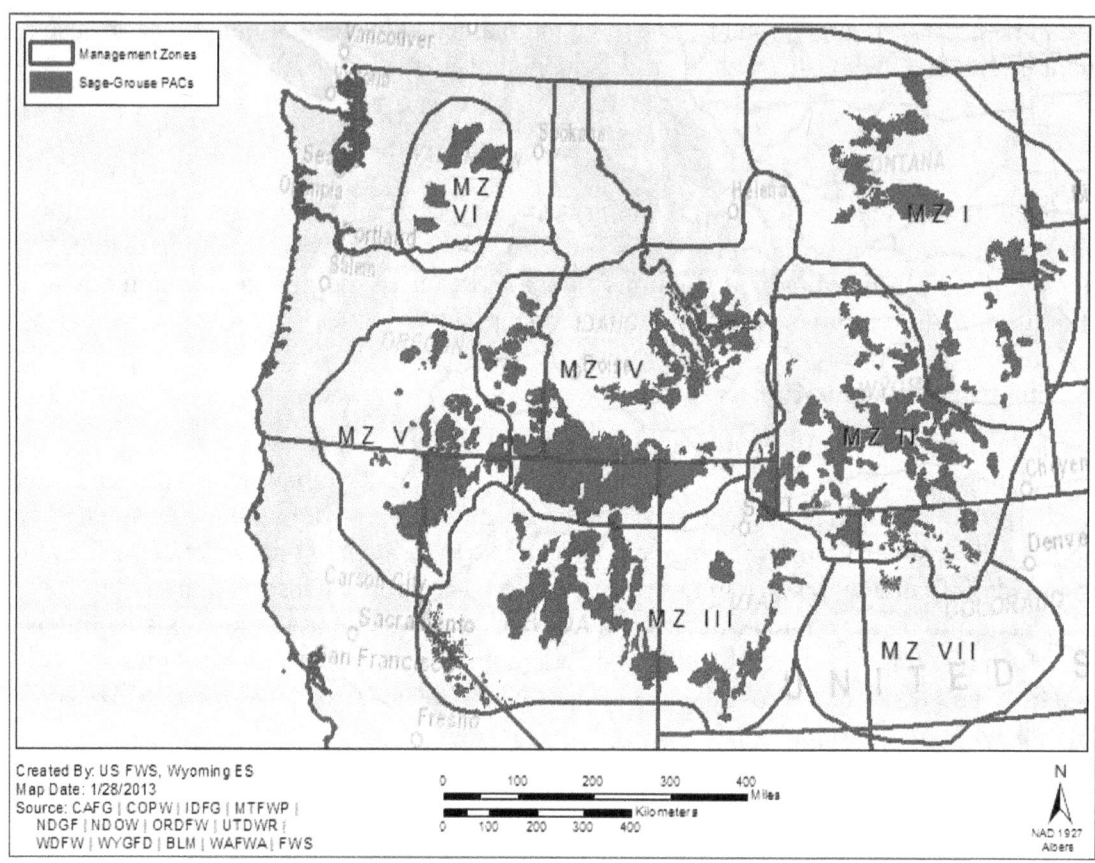

Figure 2. Sage-grouse management zones (Stiver *et al.* 2006) and Priority Areas for Conservation (PACs).

To capture the variability in threats and population resilience across the range of the sage-grouse we assessed the presence of threats to each population (Table 2) based on known occurrence of threats, existing management strategies, and professional experience. Not all threats or conservation needs are known with certainty. Areas of uncertainty include the effects of climate change and renewable energy development, the lack of robust information on population connectivity, the relationship between specific habitat characteristics and demographic parameters, and the lack of understanding of the processes necessary to restore sagebrush communities (Knick *et al.* 2003). These uncertainties do not undermine the foundation of PACs as crucial building blocks of a successful conservation strategy, but mean that some flexibility in our strategy will be necessary to retain options for the long-term conservation of the sage-grouse as new information becomes available.

Table 1. Sources of data used by states to develop Priority Areas for Conservation (PAC) maps for each state.

	CA	CO	ID	MT	ND	NV	OR	SD	UT	WA	WY
Population Based Data											
BBD/Lek Counts[a]	X	X	X	X	X	X	X		X	X	X
Telemetry	X	X	X	X		X	X	X	X	X	X
Nesting Areas	X	X		X	X	X			X	X	X
Known Distribution	X	X	X	X	X		X			X	X
Sightings/ Observations		X	X	X		X		X	X	X	X
Habitat Distribution[b]	X	X	X	X	X	X	X	X	X	X	X

[a]Breeding Bird Density (BBD) based on male counts at leks (Doherty *et al.* 2010)
[b]Habitat data included occupied habitat, suitable habitat, seasonal habitat, nesting and brood rearing areas, and connectivity areas or corridors.

Table 2. Sage-grouse quasi-extinction risk (from Garton *et al.* 2011), and threats, by management zone and population. Populations are those defined by Garton *et al.* (2011), although in some cases sub-populations were identified to help refine threat characterization (see Figure 3). Population estimates and quasi-extinction risk estimates are from Garton *et al.* (2011). Threats are characterized as: Y = threat is present and widespread, L = threat present but localized, N = threat is not known to be present, and U = Unknown.

Population	Unit Number	Population Abundance and Estimated Quasi-extinction Risk					Management Zone	Threats												
		<200 Males/500 Birds	% Chance of <50 birds/20 males in 2037	% Chance of <500 birds/200 males in 2037	% Chance of <50 birds/20 males in 2107	% Chance of <500 birds/200 males in 2107		Isolated/Small Size	Sagebrush Elimination	Agriculture Conversion	Fire	Conifers	Weeds/Annual Grasses	Energy	Mining	Infrastructure	Grazing	Free-Roaming Equids	Recreation	Urbanization
			9.5	11.1	22.8	24														
Management Zone I: Great Plains																				
Dakotas (*ND, SD*)	1	N	4.6	39.5	44.6	66.3	I	Y	L	L	Y	U	L	Y	Y	Y	L	Y	N	N
Northern Montana (*MT*)	2	N	0	0	0.2	2.0	I	N	L	L	L	N	L	Y	N	Y	Y	N	L	N
Powder River Basin (*WY*)	3	N	2.9	16.5	85.7	86.2	I	N	N	N	L	L	Y	Y	Y	Y	Y	N	Y	L

Population	Unit Number	Population Abundance and Estimated Quasi-extinction Risk					Management Zone	Threats												
		<200 Males/500 Birds	% Chance of <50 birds/ 20 males in 2037	% Chance of <500 birds/ 200 males in 2037	% Chance of <50 birds/ 20 males in 2107	% Chance of <500 birds/ 200 males in 2107		Isolated/Small Size	Sagebrush Elimination	Agriculture Conversion	Fire	Conifers	Weeds/Annual Grasses	Energy	Mining	Infrastructure	Grazing	Free-Roaming Equids	Recreation	Urbanization
Yellowstone Watershed (MT)	4	N	0	8.1	55.6	59.8	I	N	L	Y	L	L	Y	Y	N	Y	Y	N	L	N
Management Zone II: Wyoming Basin			*0.1*	*0.3*	*16.1*	*16.2*														
Eagle-South Routt (CO)	5	Y	ND	ND	ND	ND	II	Y	L	Y	L	L	Y	Y	N	Y	Y	N	L	Y
Middle Park (CO)	6	N	2.5	100	7.1	100	II	Y	Y	Y	Y	N	Y	Y	Y	Y	Y	N	Y	Y
Laramie (WY, CO)	7	N	ND	ND	ND	ND	II	Y	N	N	Y	Y	Y	Y	U	Y	Y	N	Y	Y

Population	Unit Number	<200 Males/500 Birds	% Chance of <50 birds/ 20 males in 2037	% Chance of <500 birds/ 200 males in 2037	% Chance of <50 birds/ 20 males in 2107	% Chance of <500 birds/ 200 males in 2107	Management Zone	Isolated/Small Size	Sagebrush Elimination	Agriculture Conversion	Fire	Conifers	Weeds/Annual Grasses	Energy	Mining	Infrastructure	Grazing	Free-Roaming Equids	Recreation	Urbanization
Jackson Hole (*WY*)	8	Y	11.2	100	27.3	100	II	Y	L	N	L	L	Y	N	N	N	N	N	Y	L
Wyoming Basin (*WY portion*)	9a	N					II	N	L	N	L	L	L	Y	L	Y	Y	L	Y	L
Rich-Morgan-Summit (*WY Basin in UT*)[1]	9b	N	0.0	0.0	9.9	10.7	II	N	N	N	Y	Y	Y	Y	N	Y	N	N	Y	Y
Uintah (*WY Basin in UT*)	9c	N					II	N	N	N	Y	Y	Y	L	Y	Y	N	N	Y	Y

Population	Unit Number	>200 Males/500 Birds	% Chance of <50 birds/20 males in 2037	% Chance of <500 birds/200 males in 2037	% Chance of <50 birds/20 males in 2107	% Chance of <500 birds/200 males in 2107	Management Zone	Isolated/Small Size	Sagebrush Elimination	Agriculture Conversion	Fire	Conifers	Weeds/Annual Grasses	Energy	Mining	Infrastructure	Grazing	Free-Roaming Equids	Recreation	Urbanization
N. Park (*WY Basin in CO*)	9d	N					II	N	Y	Y	Y	N	Y	Y	Y	Y	Y	N	Y	Y
NWCO (*WY Basin in CO*)	9e	N					II	N	L	Y	Y	L	Y	Y	Y	Y	Y	L	Y	L
Management Zone III: Southern Great Basin[2]			0.0	0.0	6.5	7.8														
Strawberry Valley (*Part of NE Interior UT*)	10a	Y	0.8	51.8	8.8	78.6	III	Y	N	N	Y	Y	Y	Y	N	Y	N	N	Y	N
Carbon (*Part of NE interior UT*)	10b	Y					III	Y	N	N	Y	N	Y	Y	Y	Y	N	N	Y	N

Population	Unit Number	Population Abundance and Estimated Quasi-extinction Risk					Management Zone	Threats												
		>200 Males/500 Birds	% Chance of <50 birds/20 males in 2037	% Chance of <500 birds/200 males in 2037	% Chance of <50 birds/20 males in 2107	% Chance of <500 birds/200 males in 2107		Isolated/Small Size	Sagebrush Elimination	Agriculture Conversion	Fire	Conifers	Weeds/Annual Grasses	Energy	Mining	Infrastructure	Grazing	Free-Roaming Equids	Recreation	Urbanization
Sheeprock (*UT*, aka Tooele-Juab Counties)	11	Y	56.5	100	100	100	III	Y	N	N	Y	L	L	Y	Y	L	N	Y	L	N
Emery (*UT*, aka Sanpete-Emery Counties)	12	Y	77.7	100	99.2	100	III	Y	N	N	Y	Y	Y	Y	Y	Y	N	N	Y	N
Greater Parker Mt. (*Part of South Central UT*)	13a	N	0.0	3.2	1.1	21.0	III	N	N	N	Y	Y	Y	N	N	Y	N	N	Y	N

Population	Unit Number	Population Abundance and Estimated Quasi-extinction Risk					Management Zone	Threats												
		<200 Males/500 Birds	% Chance of <50 birds/ 20 males in 2037	% Chance of <500 birds/ 200 males in 2037	% Chance of <50 birds/ 20 males in 2107	% Chance of <500 birds/ 200 males in 2107		Isolated/Small Size	Sagebrush Elimination	Agriculture Conversion	Fire	Conifers	Weeds/Annual Grasses	Energy	Mining	Infrastructure	Grazing	Free-Roaming Equids	Recreation	Urbanization
Panguitch (*Part of South Central UT*)	13b	N					III	N	N	Y	Y	Y	Y	Y	L	Y	N	N	Y	L
Bald Hills (*Part of South Central UT*)	13c	Y					III	Y	N	Y	Y	Y	Y	Y	Y	Y	N	Y	Y	Y
Northwest Interior (*NV*)	14	N	ND	ND	ND	ND	III	Y	N	N	Y	N	Y	U	Y	Y	Y	Y	Y	N
Ibapah (*UT part of Southern Great Basin*)	15a	Y	0.0	2.0	4.2	78.0	III	Y	N	N	Y	Y	Y	Y	Y	Y	N	Y	Y	N

Population	Unit Number	Population Abundance and Estimated Quasi-extinction Risk					Management Zone	Threats												
		<200 Males/500 Birds	% Chance of <50 birds/20 males in 2037	% Chance of <500 birds/200 males in 2037	% Chance of <50 birds/20 males in 2107	% Chance of <500 birds/200 males in 2107		Isolated/Small Size	Sagebrush Elimination	Agriculture Conversion	Fire	Conifers	Weeds/Annual Grasses	Energy	Mining	Infrastructure	Grazing	Free-Roaming Equids	Recreation	Urbanization
Hamlin Valley (*UT part of Southern Great Basin*)	15b	Y					III	Y	N	N	Y	Y	Y	N	N	Y	N	Y	Y	N
Southern Great Basin (*NV portion*)	15c	N					III	L	L	L	Y	Y	Y	L	L	L	Y	Y	Y	N
Quinn Canyon Range (*NV*)	16	Y	ND	ND	ND	ND	III	Y	N	N	Y	Y	Y	N	N	Y	Y	Y	Y	N
Management Zone IV: Snake River Plains			*2.3*	*10.5*	*19.4*	*39.7*														
Baker (*OR*)	17	N	61.9	100	66.8	100	IV	Y	Y	Y	Y	Y	Y	L	Y	L	N	U	L	L

Population	Unit Number	Population Abundance and Estimated Quasi-extinction Risk					Management Zone	Threats												
		>200 Males/500 Birds	% Chance of <50 birds/ 20 males in 2037	% Chance of <500 birds/ 200 males in 2037	% Chance of <50 birds/ 20 males in 2107	% Chance of <500 birds/ 200 males in 2107		Isolated/Small Size	Sagebrush Elimination	Agriculture Conversion	Fire	Conifers	Weeds/Annual Grasses	Energy	Mining	Infrastructure	Grazing	Free-Roaming Equids	Recreation	Urbanization
East Central (ID)	18	Y	ND	ND	ND	ND	IV	Y	L	Y	L	Y	L	Y	N	Y	Y	N	L	N
Southwest Montana (Bannack, Red Rocks, Wisdom, and Bridges)	19-22	N	Bannack: 6.4 Red Rock: 0.1	Bannack: 70.2 Red Rock: 55.3	Bannack: 32.7 Red Rock: 2.5	Bannack: 97.7 Red Rock: 91.9	IV	N	L	N	L	L	Y	L	L	L	Y	N	L	L
Snake-Salmon-Beaverhead (ID)	23	N	4.2	10.2	19.3	26.8	IV	N	L	L	Y	L	Y	Y	N	L	Y	Y	L	N
Belt Mountains (MT)	24	Y	ND	ND	ND	ND	IV	Y	L	Y	L	L	Y	L	N	L	Y	N	L	L

Population	Unit Number	Population Abundance and Estimated Quasi-extinction Risk					Management Zone	Threats												
		>200 Males/500 Birds	% Chance of <50 birds/ 20 males in 2037	% Chance of <500 birds/ 200 males in 2037	% Chance of <50 birds/ 20 males in 2107	% Chance of <500 birds/ 200 males in 2107		Isolated/Small Size	Sagebrush Elimination	Agriculture Conversion	Fire	Conifers	Weeds/Annual Grasses	Energy	Mining	Infrastructure	Grazing	Free-Roaming Equids	Recreation	Urbanization
Weiser (*ID*)	25	N	ND	ND	ND	ND	IV	Y	L	L	L	L	Y	Y	N	L	Y	N	L	L
Northern Great Basin (*OR, ID, NV portion*)	26a	N	2.1	2.5	2.5	99.7	IV	N	L	L	Y	Y	Y	L	L	Y	Y	L	Y	Y
Box Elder (*UT portion of Northern Great Basin*)	26b	N					IV	N	N	Y	Y	Y	Y	L	Y	Y	N	N	Y	N
Sawtooth (*ID*)	27	Y	ND	ND	ND	ND	IV	Y	L	N	L	L	L	N	N	Y	Y	N	L	N

Management Zone V: Northern Great Basin

Population	Unit Number	<200 Males/500 Birds	% Chance of <50 birds/20 males in 2037 (1.0)	% Chance of <500 birds/200 males in 2037 (2.1)	% Chance of <50 birds/20 males in 2107 (7.2)	% Chance of <500 birds/200 males in 2107 (29)	Management Zone	Isolated/Small Size	Sagebrush Elimination	Agriculture Conversion	Fire	Conifers	Weeds/Annual Grasses	Energy	Mining	Infrastructure	Grazing	Free-Roaming Equids	Recreation	Urbanization
Central Oregon (*OR*)	28	N	4.2	15.2	74.9	91.3	V	N	L	L	Y	Y	Y	L	Y	L	Y	U	L	L
Klamath (*OR, CA*)	29	Y	ND	ND	100	100	V	Y	U	U	Y	Y	Y	L	N	U	U	U	U	U
Warm Springs Valley (*NV*)	30	Y	ND	ND	ND	ND	V	Y	N	Y	Y	Y	Y	Y	N	Y	Y	Y	Y	Y

Population	Unit Number	Population Abundance and Estimated Quasi-extinction Risk					Management Zone	Threats												
		<200 Males/500 Birds	% Chance of <50 birds/ 20 males in 2037	% Chance of <500 birds/ 200 males in 2037	% Chance of <50 birds/ 20 males in 2107	% Chance of <500 birds/ 200 males in 2107		Isolated/Small Size	Sagebrush Elimination	Agriculture Conversion	Fire	Conifers	Weeds/Annual Grasses	Energy	Mining	Infrastructure	Grazing	Free-Roaming Equids	Recreation	Urbanization
Western Great Basin (*OR, CA, NV*)	31	N	5.5	6.4	6.4	99.1	V	N	L	L	Y	Y	Y	L	L	L	Y	Y	U	N
Management Zone VI: Columbia Basin			12.4	76.2	62.1	86.3														
Moses Coulee (*WA*)	32a	N	9.8	87.6	62.4	99.8	VI	Y	Y	Y	L	N	Y	Y	N	Y	Y	N	Y	Y
Crab Creek (*WA*)	32b	Y	ND	ND	ND	ND	VI	Y	Y	Y	Y	L	L	Y	N	Y	Y	N	Y	L

Population	Unit Number	Population Abundance and Estimated Quasi-extinction Risk					Management Zone	Isolated/Small Size	Sagebrush Elimination	Agriculture Conversion	Fire	Conifers	Weeds/Annual Grasses	Energy	Mining	Infrastructure	Grazing	Free-Roaming Equids	Recreation	Urbanization
		>200 Males/500 Birds	% Chance of <50 birds/ 20 males in 2037	% Chance of <500 birds/ 200 males in 2037	% Chance of <50 birds/ 20 males in 2107	% Chance of <500 birds/ 200 males in 2107														
Yakama Indian Nation (WA)	33a	Y	ND	ND	ND	ND	VI	Y	N	N	Y	N	Y	Y	N	Y	Y	Y	Y	L
Yakima Training Center (WA)	33b	Y	26.1	100	50.4	100	VI	Y	N	L	Y	N	Y	N	N	Y	Y	N	Y	N
Management Zone VII: Colorado Plateau			0.0	95.6	5.1	98.4														
Parachute-Piceance-Roan Basin (CO)	34	Y	ND	ND	ND	ND	VII	Y	L	N	N	Y	L	Y	Y	Y	Y	Y	N	N

Population	Unit Number	Population Abundance and Estimated Quasi-extinction Risk					Management Zone	Threats												
		>200 Males/500 Birds	% Chance of <50 birds/ 20 males in 2037	% Chance of <500 birds/ 200 males in 2037	% Chance of <50 birds/ 20 males in 2107	% Chance of <500 birds/ 200 males in 2107		Isolated/Small Size	Sagebrush Elimination	Agriculture Conversion	Fire	Conifers	Weeds/Annual Grasses	Energy	Mining	Infrastructure	Grazing	Free-Roaming Equids	Recreation	Urbanization
Meeker-White River (CO)	35	Y	ND	ND	ND	ND	VII	Y	Y	Y	Y	N	L	L	Y	Y	Y	N	N	Y
Bi-State Distinct Population Segment																				
North Mono Lake (CA, NV)	36	N	15.4	100	37.9	100	III	Y	L	Y	Y	Y	Y	L	Y	Y	Y	Y	Y	Y
South Mono Lake (CA)	37	N	0.1	81.5	0.6	99.9	III	Y	Y	Y	Y	Y	Y	N	N	Y	Y	Y	Y	Y
Pine Nut (NV)	38	Y	ND	ND	ND	ND	III	Y	L	U	U	Y	Y	N	L	L	Y	Y	Y	Y

| Population | Unit Number | Population Abundance and Estimated Quasi-extinction Risk | | | | | Management Zone | Threats | | | | | | | | | | | | |
		<200 Males/500 Birds	% Chance of <50 birds/ 20 males in 2037	% Chance of <500 birds/ 200 males in 2037	% Chance of <50 birds/ 20 males in 2107	% Chance of <500 birds/ 200 males in 2107		Isolated/Small Size	Sagebrush Elimination	Agriculture Conversion	Fire	Conifers	Weeds/Annual Grasses	Energy	Mining	Infrastructure	Grazing	Free-Roaming Equids	Recreation	Urbanization
White Mountains (CA, NV)	39	Y	ND	ND	ND	ND	III	Y	L	Y	Y	Y	Y	N	N	Y	Y	Y	U	Y

[1] This UT management area includes Summit-Morgan Counties, which is described separately by Garton *et al.* (2011) as a subpopulation in Management Zone III. Numbers for columns 4-7 for this population are 20.6, 100, 41.8, and 100, respectively (Garton *et al.* 2011).

[2] Percentages reported in this zone by Garton *et al.* (2011) include information for North and South Mono Lake, which are separately described in the Bi-State section of this table.

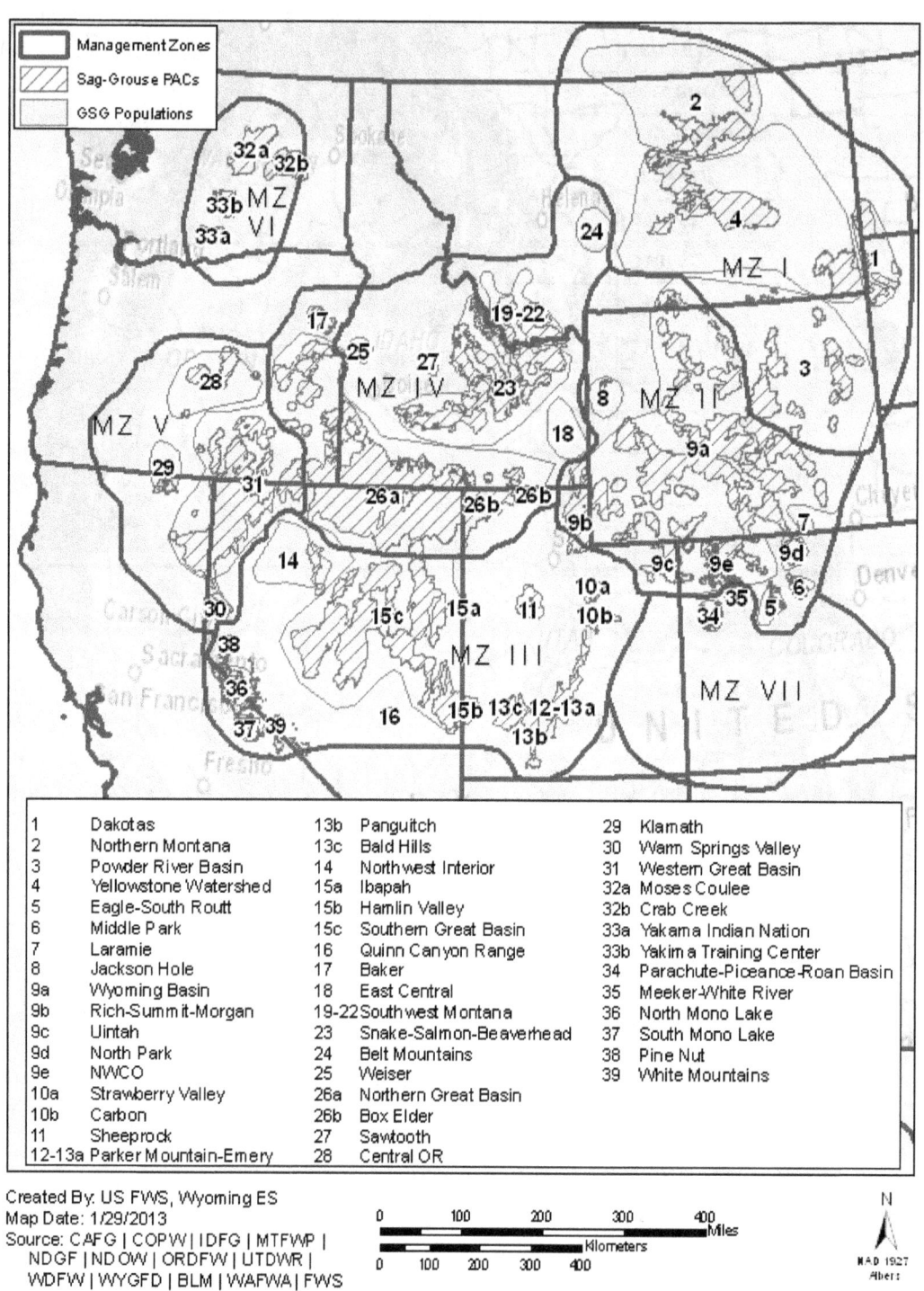

Figure 3. Sage-grouse management zones (Stiver *et al.* 2006), populations (adapted from Garton *et al.* 2011), and Priority Areas for Conservation (PACs; see Section 4.3). Threats to the populations identified here are described in Table 2.

The following legend and labels appear within the map figure:

Management Zones
Sag-Grouse PACs
GSG Populations

1	Dakotas	13b	Panguitch	29	Klamath
2	Northern Montana	13c	Bald Hills	30	Warm Springs Valley
3	Powder River Basin	14	Northwest Interior	31	Western Great Basin
4	Yellowstone Watershed	15a	Ibapah	32a	Moses Coulee
5	Eagle-South Routt	15b	Hamlin Valley	32b	Crab Creek
6	Middle Park	15c	Southern Great Basin	33a	Yakama Indian Nation
7	Laramie	16	Quinn Canyon Range	33b	Yakima Training Center
8	Jackson Hole	17	Baker	34	Parachute-Piceance-Roan Basin
9a	Wyoming Basin	18	East Central	35	Meeker-White River
9b	Rich-Summit-Morgan	19-22	Southwest Montana	36	North Mono Lake
9c	Uintah	23	Snake-Salmon-Beaverhead	37	South Mono Lake
9d	North Park	24	Belt Mountains	38	Pine Nut
9e	NWCO	25	Weiser	39	White Mountains
10a	Strawberry Valley	26a	Northern Great Basin		
10b	Carbon	26b	Box Elder		
11	Sheeprock	27	Sawtooth		
12-13a	Parker Mountain-Emery	28	Central OR		

Created By: US FWS, Wyoming ES
Map Date: 1/29/2013
Source: CAFG | COPW | IDFG | MTFWP | NDGF | NDOW | ORDFW | UTDWR | WDFW | WYGFD | BLM | WAFWA | FWS

N
NAD 1927
Albers

5. CONSERVATION OBJECTIVES

The conservation objectives identified below are targeted at maintaining redundant, representative, and resilient sage-grouse habitats and populations. Due to the variability in ecological conditions and the nature of the threats across the range of the sage-grouse, developing detailed, prescriptive species or habitat actions is not possible at the range-wide scale. Specific strategies or actions necessary to achieve the following conservation objectives must be developed and implemented at the state or local level, with the involvement of all stakeholders.

In developing conservation objectives for the sage-grouse we identified the following uncertainties that limit our ability to prescribe a precise level of threat amelioration needed to conserve redundancy, representation and resilience to ensure long-term conservation of sage-grouse, especially on a range-wide level:

1. The lack of robust, range-wide genetics-based connectivity analyses;

2. The ability to successfully restore lower-elevation and weed-infested habitats is currently limited by a lack of complete understanding of underlying ecological processes, and in some areas because alteration of vegetation, nutrient cycles, topsoil, and living (cryptobiotic) soil crusts has exceeded recovery thresholds (Knick *et al.* 2003; Pyke 2011). Additionally, resources for restoration activities are often limited; and,

3. The effect of climate change on the amount and distribution of future habitat is largely unknown.

In light of these significant uncertainties, impacts to sage-grouse and their habitats should be avoided to the maximum extent possible to retain conservation options. This approach will ensure that potentially unidentified key components to long-term viability of sage-grouse are not lost, and that management flexibility and the ability to implement management changes will be retained as current information gaps are filled. Implementing an avoidance first strategy should reduce or avoid continuing declines of sage-grouse populations and habitats, as well as limit further reduction in management and restoration options. When avoidance is not possible, meaningful minimization and mitigation of the impacts should be implemented, along with a monitoring program to evaluate the efficacy of these measures. Conservation measures should be adapted to maximize effectiveness as new knowledge is obtained.

General Conservation Objectives

1. *Stop population declines and habitat loss.* There is an urgent need to "stop the bleeding" of continued population declines and habitat losses by acting immediately to eliminate or reduce the impacts contributing to population declines and range erosion. There are no

populations within the range of sage-grouse that are immune to the threat of habitat loss and fragmentation.

a) Achieving this objective requires eliminating activities known to negatively impact sage-grouse and their habitats, or re-designing these activities to achieve the same goal. As described in our 2010 warranted but precluded finding (75 FR 13910, and references therein), local sage-grouse extirpations and habitat losses have already reduced management (and therefore recovery) options in some portions of the species' range (e.g. the Columbia Basin, Washington). Further, many populations are declining (WAFWA 2008; Garton *et al.* 2011) due to past and ongoing habitat loss, degradation and fragmentation, and many face significant threats (Table 2), or are inherently challenged by current population size (as discussed in section 4, above). Implementing an avoidance first strategy should minimize continuing declines in the species and its habitats, as well as limit further reduction in management options.

b) The appropriate level of management must continue to effectively conserve all current PACs. Threats in PACs must be minimized to the extent that population trends meet the objectives of the 2006 WAFWA Conservation Strategy (Stiver *et al.* 2006; see discussion regarding specific threat amelioration objectives below). Additionally, PACs should be managed to maintain, and improve degraded habitats to provide healthy intact sagebrush shrub and native perennial grass and forb communities, appropriate to the local ecological conditions, and to conserve all essential seasonal habitat components for sage-grouse.

2. *Implement targeted habitat management and restoration.* Some sage-grouse populations warrant more than the amelioration of the impacts from stressors to maintain sage-grouse on the landscape. In these instances, and particularly with impacts resulting from wildfire, it may be critical to not only remove or reduce anthropogenic threats to these populations but additionally to improve population health through active habitat management (e.g. habitat restoration). This is particularly important for those populations that are essential to maintaining range-wide redundancy and representation.

a) Removal of all threats may not be sufficient to change the status of some populations, as some of these populations (and associated PACs) are subject to non-anthropogenic threats (e.g., lighting-caused fires) or may have already declined to a point where active management is required for their long-term viability (e.g., Clear Lake area of northern California). In these cases, proactive management of non-anthropogenic threats (e.g., strategic placement of fire-fighting resources) and restoration efforts should be implemented.

b) The effectiveness of restoration activities (ultimately determined by sage-grouse use and population trends) must be demonstrated prior to receiving any credit for mitigating losses. Restoration activities should be developed within a framework that allows for necessary adjustments.

c) Effective habitat conservation and, as appropriate, restoration activities, should be implemented immediately. The typically long response times of sagebrush ecosystems to most management activities necessitates that these activities be initiated so that their results can be considered for long-term conservation strategies. Development and Implementation of monitoring plans for these activities is an essential component of these efforts.

d) Some areas that were not included as PACs may still have great potential for providing important habitat if active habitat management is implemented. For example, removal of early-stage juniper stands may render currently unsuitable habitat into effective habitat for sage-grouse (this is also true for degraded habitats within PACs). State and federal agencies should actively pursue these opportunities. Successful habitat management efforts could increase connectivity between PACs, and will enhance management flexibility in conserving the species.

3. *Develop and implement state and federal sage-grouse conservation strategies and associated incentive-based conservation actions and regulatory mechanisms.* To conserve sage-grouse and habitat redundancy, representation, and resilience, state and federal agencies, along with interested stakeholders within range of the sage-grouse should work together to develop a plan, including any necessary regulatory or legal tools (or use an existing plan, if appropriate) that includes clear mechanisms for addressing the threats to sage-grouse within PACs. Where consistent with state conservation plans, sage-grouse habitats outside of PACs should also be addressed. We recognize that threats can be ameliorated through a variety of tools within the purview of states and federal agencies, including incentive-based conservation actions or regulatory mechanisms. Federal land management agencies should work with states in developing adequate regulatory mechanisms. Federal land management agencies should also contribute to the incentive-based conservation and habitat restoration and rehabilitation efforts. In the development of conservation plans, entities (states, federal land management agencies, etc.) should coordinate with FWS. This will ensure that the plans address the threats contributing to the 2010 warranted but precluded determination, and that conservation strategies will meaningfully contribute to future listing analyses.

   a) Successful implementation of regulatory and incentive-based mechanisms to conserve sage-grouse requires that all stakeholders participate in conservation, regardless of the size, type, ownership, or location of the threat impact. Continued losses by controllable individual activities of any size can result in significant impacts to the conservation of the species when considered cumulatively, and these losses also reduce management options.

   b) Sage-grouse conservation strategies should consider using the criteria identified in the FWS/NOAA Fisheries *Policy for Evaluation of Conservation Efforts (PECE) when Making Listing Decisions* (Federal Register/Vol. 68, No. 60/Friday, March

28, 2003; Appendix B) to help evaluate its likely implementation and effectiveness.

    i.   Conservation plans should:

        1. Be based on the best available science;

        2. Use local data on threats and ecological conditions, including status of local sage-grouse populations and their associated habitats;

        3. Maintain the diversity of sagebrush habitats essential to provide for all sage-grouse seasonal and life history stages;

        4. Maintain genetic and physical connectivity; and,

        5. Maintain all current intact sage-grouse habitats according to the state management plans (developed in coordination with FWS as discussed above) or other conservation efforts (e.g., BLM priority areas), recognizing existing valid rights.

    ii.   Conservation plans should be completed no later than July 2013 for the Bi-State DPS, and September of 2014 for the rest of the species' range.

c) Regulatory mechanisms must be completed and implemented and incentive-based conservation actions negotiated as quickly as possible (no later than July 2013 for the Bi-State DPS and September 2014 for the rest of the sage-grouse range, including the Columbia Basin DPS). The effectiveness of regulatory mechanisms and incentive-based conservation activities will be assessed on whether such efforts will successfully ameliorate the specific threats associated with each population and its' associated PACs (See Table 2 in Part 5). Regulatory mechanisms and incentive-based actions should address all threats to PACs to the maximum extent practicable.

d) If adequate regulatory mechanisms cannot be implemented prior to July 2013 for the Bi-State DPS, and Sept. 2014 for the species across the rest of its range, then enforceable temporary measures should be considered in order to ensure threats will be at least temporarily ameliorated until such time that an effective regulatory mechanism can be implemented.

e) All regulatory and incentive-based mechanisms should have a monitoring plan that will provide scientifically defensible data regarding their effectiveness. New or adapted mechanisms must be developed and implemented if monitoring determines that current regulatory mechanisms are ineffective.

4. *Develop and implement proactive, voluntary conservation actions.* Proactive, incentive-based, voluntary conservation actions (e.g. Candidate Conservation Agreements with Assurances, Natural Resources Conservation Service programs) should be developed and/or implemented by interested stakeholders and closely coordinated across the range of the species to ensure they are complimentary and address sage-grouse conservation needs and threats. These efforts need to receive full funding, including funding for necessary personnel.

Many stakeholders within the sagebrush ecosystem have been working diligently to proactively minimize the impacts of their projects on the sage-grouse. Currently, proactive voluntary conservation actions for sage-grouse are being implemented in many parts of the species' range. Given the vast extent of the species' range implementation of voluntary conservation actions may not provide all actions necessary for conservation of the species range-wide. Nevertheless, the combination of voluntary efforts and active management by state and federal agencies via habitat improvements and governmental regulatory mechanisms could have a significant influence on the Service's upcoming listing determinations. These combined actions should apply to the activities which cause habitat fragmentation and loss, the primary factor identified in the FWS 2010 warranted but precluded finding. Stakeholders engaged in voluntary conservation actions should collect information on the geographic scope of these efforts, the sustained benefits to sage-grouse from their implementation, and the likelihood that they will continue to be implemented in the future. This information will be essential to informing the FWS listing decisions.

    a) Funding and other necessary support for current proactive conservation efforts should be continued.

    b) All proactive voluntary conservation efforts should use the best available science to develop and implement management actions. The results of these efforts should be tracked and reported annually. To monitor effectiveness, these efforts should have a monitoring plan which will provide the necessary scientifically-based information that allows for modification if necessary to achieve the conservation objective.

5. *Develop and implement monitoring plans to track the success of state and federal conservation strategies and voluntary conservation actions.* A robust range-wide monitoring program must be developed and implemented for sage-grouse conservation plans, which recognizes and incorporates individual state approaches. A monitoring program is necessary to track the success of conservation plans and proactive conservation activities. Without this information, the actual benefit of conservation activities cannot be measured and there is no capacity to adapt if current management actions are determined to be ineffective.

    a) Adequate funding must be secured for development, implementation, and enforcement of regulatory and incentive-based mechanisms, other conservation strategies, and monitoring programs.

    b) New or adapted management actions must be developed and implemented if the monitoring determines that current management actions are ineffective.

6. *Prioritize, fund, and implement research to address existing uncertainties.* Increased funding and support for key research projects that will address uncertainties associated with sage-grouse and sagebrush habitat management is essential. Effective amelioration

of threats can only be accomplished if the mechanisms by which those threats are imposed on the redundancy, representation, and resilience of the species and its habitats are understood.

Specific Conservation Objectives

Priority Areas for Conservation (PACs)

Delineation of key sage-grouse habitats recognizes the extensive reach of habitat threats, the existing loss and degradation of habitats, and acknowledges that preservation of every remaining area of sage-grouse habitat is improbable (Kiesecker *et al.* 2011). Priority Areas for Conservation (PACs) are key habitats identified by state sage-grouse conservation plans (for each state that has such a plan), or through other sage-grouse conservation efforts (e.g. the current BLM planning effort for greater sage-grouse). Maintenance of the integrity of PACs (i.e., maintenance of a healthy sagebrush shrub and native perennial grass and forb community appropriate to local site ecological conditions, which conserves all essential habitat components for sage-grouse) is the essential foundation for sage-grouse conservation. Threats in PACs must be minimized as part of the effort to meet the objectives of the 2006 WAFWA Conservation Strategy (Stiver *et al.* 2006). These objectives include reversing negative population trends within each Management Zone **and** achieving a positive or neutral population trend, with long-term success assessed by comparison with trend data from 1965 – 2003 for each Management Zone. Application of the following conservation objectives (as applicable to local conditions) is unlikely to result in immediate, detectable changes in sage-grouse population trends. However, incorporation of these objectives into conservation planning efforts, including rigorous monitoring plans, will help provide the assurance that the long-term population trend objectives are likely to be attained.

Sage-grouse habitats outside of PACs may also be essential, by providing connectivity between PACs (genetic and habitat linkages), habitat restoration and population expansion opportunities, and flexibility for managing habitat changes that may result from climate change. There may also be seasonal habitats outside of PACs essential to meeting the year-round needs of sage-grouse within PACs but that have not yet been identified. Therefore, maintaining habitats outside of PACs may be important (Fedy *et al.* 2012). Conservation of sage-grouse habitats outside of the PACs should be closely coordinated with each state. For those states with sage-grouse management plans, or similar documents adequately addressing the conservation of sage-grouse that have been developed in coordination with FWS, decisions on management of those areas should defer to those plans. Conservation of habitats outside of PACs should include minimization of impacts to sage-grouse and healthy native plant communities. If minimization is not possible due to valid existing rights, mitigation for impacted habitats should occur.

Loss of PACs (e.g., through wildfire) will reduce the long-term viability of the greater sage-grouse and its habitats. The precise impact of the loss of a PAC, or part of a PAC, to the long-term conservation of sage-grouse cannot be predicted, as the impact will depend on location and size of the PAC and the extent of habitat lost. Nevertheless loss of a PAC, or significant reduction in available habitat within a PAC, will reduce redundancy and representation across the sage-grouse range, thereby increasing the risk of local extirpation, loss of population connectivity, and reducing management options. Therefore, it is imperative that no PACs are lost as a result of further infrastructure development or other anthropogenic impacts.

The following objectives are targeted at conserving PACs, but can be applied to sage-grouse habitats outside of PACs. These objectives apply to both the Bi-State DPS and sage-grouse range-wide. Achieving these objectives will conserve redundancy and representation of the species and its habitats across its range.

1. Retain sage-grouse habitats within PACs. This must be a priority. Restoration of these habitats, once lost, is difficult, expensive, and based on current knowledge, success may be limited.

2. If PACs are lost to catastrophic events, implement appropriate restoration efforts (Pyke 2011). Given that adequate restoration is often very difficult and takes many years, in addition to restoration, efforts should be made to restore the components lost within the PAC (e.g., redundancy or representation) in other areas such that there is no net loss of sage-grouse or their habitats.

3. Restore and rehabilitate degraded sage-grouse habitats in PACs. This will require sufficient funding and resources, a scientifically rigorous monitoring plan, and the ability to change management if the monitoring results so indicate.

4. Identify areas and habitats outside of PACs which may be necessary to maintain the viability of sage-grouse. If development or vegetation manipulation activities outside of PACs are proposed, the project proponent should work with federal, state or local agencies and interested stakeholders to ensure consistency with sage-grouse habitat needs.

5. Re-evaluate the status of PACs and adjacent sage-grouse habitat at least once every 5 years, or when important new information becomes available (e.g. identification of a previously unknown important winter habitat area). PAC boundaries should be adjusted based on new information regarding habitat suitability and refined mapping techniques, new genetic connectivity information, and new or updated information on seasonal range delineation. By maintaining current maps of the habitat areas necessary to provide redundancy and representation, conservation plans can be more accurately implemented, or modified if appropriate. Additionally, new restoration or rehabilitation opportunities may be identified, thereby increasing management flexibility. Basing management decisions on out-of-date data or natural resource dogma (Beck *et al.* 2012) may threaten the success of long-term conservation actions and conservation plans.

6. Actively pursue opportunities to increase occupancy and connectivity between PACs. Some areas that were not included as PACs may still have great potential for providing important habitat if active habitat management is implemented.

7. Maintain or improve existing habitat conditions in areas adjacent to burned habitat. In the late summer of 2012, several large wildfires in the Great Basin burned through sage-grouse habitats, including PACs (Figure 3). Significant sage-grouse habitat losses were sustained in PACs across California, Nevada, Idaho and Oregon, and in PACs that border those state boundaries. Acreage within fire perimeters in PACs total 265,151 acres in California, 486,293 acres in Nevada, 286,820 acres in Idaho, and 695,619 acres in Oregon. The resulting, immediate loss of habitat raises concerns for the capacity of at least some of those PACs to sustain sage-grouse populations. The unburned portions of these PACs cannot tolerate further impacts to sage-grouse without risking additional population declines. Funding for restoration activities to restore habitat and connectivity in these areas must be a priority. Minimizing or eliminating anthropogenic activities in surrounding, unburned PACs and sage-grouse habitats outside of PACs must also be a priority to enhance opportunities for re-establishment of connectivity among populations, and subsequent re-colonization of restored areas. Management actions within those surrounding PACs must strive to maintain or improve existing habitat conditions so that when a fire occurs, there is a greater chance for successful habitat recovery. Research to understand sage-grouse response to these fires should be prioritized so that any appropriate management modifications, including the modification or addition of PACs, can be implemented.

Threat Reduction

The following threat reduction objectives and measures are targeted at the habitat threats facing the greater sage-grouse, as identified in the 2010 warranted but precluded finding (75 FR 13910). Successful achievement of these objectives across the species' range will ameliorate the threats to greater sage-grouse, including the Bi-State DPS, and allow for the long-term conservation of the species. In the development of conservation plans to achieve these threat reduction objectives, entities (states, federal land management agencies, etc.) should coordinate with FWS. This will help to ensure that the conservation plans adequately address the threats contributing to the 2010 warranted but precluded finding.

The March 2010 finding determined that the greater sage-grouse was warranted for listing based on two primary factors – the present or threatened destruction, modification or curtailment of habitat or range, and the inadequacy of existing regulatory mechanisms. The following strategies addressing resilience are therefore focused on the first listing factor – habitat. In many situations adequate regulatory mechanisms are essential to addressing habitat concerns. The adequacy of regulatory mechanisms is being addressed via several other venues, including the land management planning that the FS and BLM are engaged in and the development and implementation of individual state management plans. Other factors may have local impacts on sage-grouse and state management plans developed in coordination with FWS should provide a basis for addressing these concerns. However, because those other factors did not rise to the level of warranting a listing range-wide (e.g., disease), they are not addressed in this report. Resolution of the habitat concerns discussed below will assist in addressing these other local factors and therefore, these efforts are not mutually exclusive.

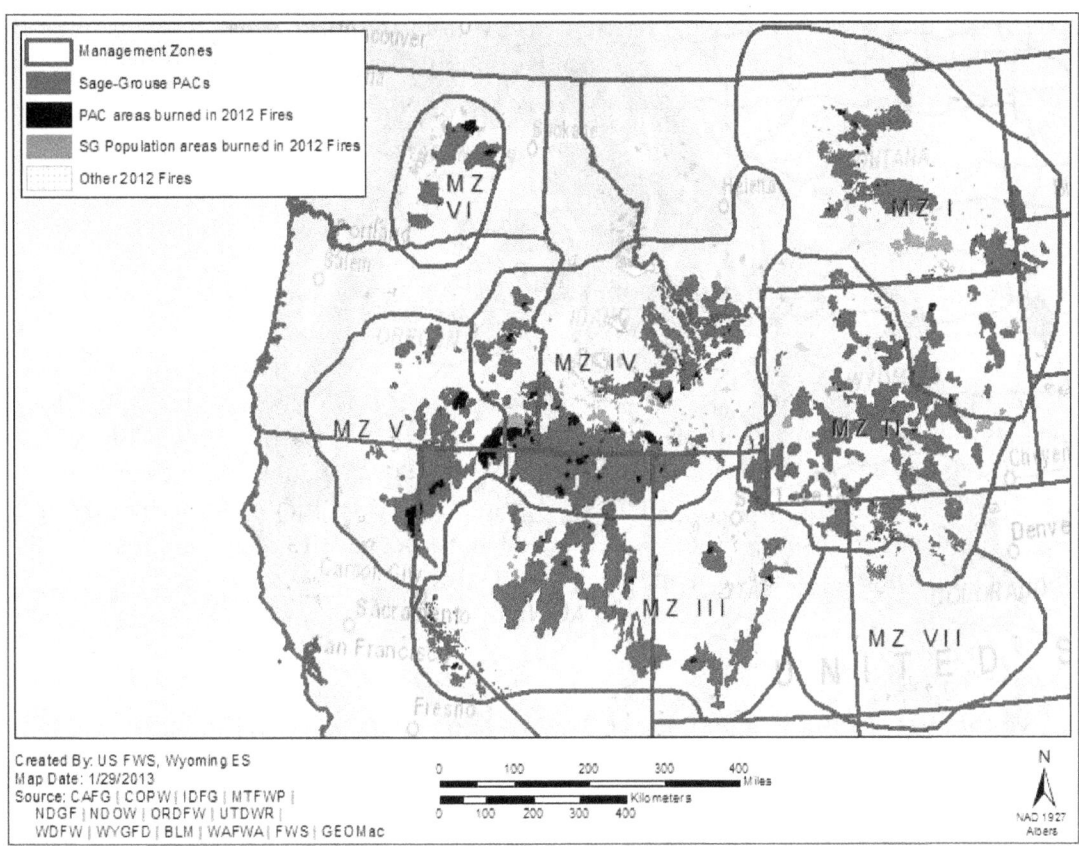

Figure 4. Sage-grouse management zones (Stiver *et al.* 2006), Priority Areas for Conservation (PACs), and 2012 fire perimeters within or near sage-grouse populations. Areas in black indicate areas of PACs that burned while areas in orange indicate areas within the range of sage-grouse, but outside of PACs that burned.

In instances where local data are available for addressing any of the objectives outlined below, they should be used. Where local data are not available information from peer-reviewed literature and rigorous scientific studies should be used to develop local management targets (e.g. amount of understory cover necessary to improve nesting success).

Brief summaries of the impacts of each habitat threat described below are provided as a general reference only. The March, 2010 listing determination (75 FR 13910) provides more detailed analyses of these threats. In addition to identifying conservation objectives associated with each threat we also provide conservation measures that are likely to help achieve that objective. For some threats, examples of options to assist in achieving the conservation objective are also provided for consideration. We did not identify objectives for addressing the potential impacts of climate change due to the uncertainties associated with modeling the resulting future condition and distribution of sage-brush habitats. However, conservation plans should consider climate change models, using local data when available, in the management of sage-grouse habitats.

The following objectives apply to PACs, but all opportunities to reduce threats within sage-grouse habitats should be considered. Where conservation actions are essential outside of PACs, it is noted in the objectives below. These objectives apply to both the Bi-State DPS, and sage-grouse range-wide.

Fire

Conservation Objective: Retain and restore healthy native sagebrush plant communities within the range of sage-grouse.

Fire (both lightning-caused and human-caused fire) in sagebrush ecosystems is one of the primary risks to the greater sage-grouse, especially as part of the positive feedback loop between exotic invasive annual grasses and fire frequency. As the replacement of native perennial bunchgrass communities by invasive annuals is a primary contributing factor to increasing fire frequencies in the sagebrush ecosystem, every effort must be made to retain and restore this native plant community, both within and outside of PACs.

Conservation Measures:

1. Restrict or contain fire within the normal range of fire activity (assuming a healthy native perennial sagebrush community), including size and frequency, as defined by the best available science.
2. Eliminate intentional fires in sagebrush habitats, including prescribed burning of breeding and winter habitats.
3. Design and implement restoration of burned sagebrush habitats to allow for natural succession to healthy native sagebrush plant communities. This will necessitate an intensive and well-funded monitoring system for this long-term endeavor. To be considered successful, restoration must also result in returning or increasing sage-grouse populations within burned areas.
4. Implement monitoring programs for restoration activities. To ensure success, monitoring must continue until restoration is complete (establishment of mature, healthy native sagebrush plant communities), with sufficient commitments to make adequate corrections to management efforts if needed.
5. Immediately suppress fire in all sagebrush habitats. Where resources are limited, these actions should first focus on PACs and any identified connectivity corridors between PACs.

Threat reduction for fire is difficult and costly. Given the intensity and wide distribution of this threat it may never be fully addressed. However implementing the suite of conservation measures listed above is likely to significantly reduce the impact of fire on the long-term viability of the sage-grouse.

Addressing fire, and subsequent successful restoration activities, in sagebrush ecosystems will require consideration of local ecological conditions, which cannot be prescribed on a range-wide level. Where state sage-grouse management plans already provide an effective strategy for fire, the COT defers to those efforts. In all other situations, the following options should be considered in developing a fire management strategy. Specific strategies for reducing the threat of fire should be drafted by July 2013 for the Bi-State population and by September 2014 for sage-grouse rangewide, and should consider the criteria outlined in the PECE policy (Appendix B).

Conservation Options:

1. Prevention of fires in sage-grouse habitats
   a. Manage for the maintenance and, where necessary, restoration of healthy perennial grass (Blank and Morgan 2012) and sagebrush vegetative communities.
   b. Manage land uses (e.g., improper livestock grazing, OHV and recreational use, roads) to minimize the spread of invasive species and or facilitate fire ignition.
   c. Address degraded sagebrush systems before fire occurs (e.g., improve grazing systems).
   d. Close rangelands that are highly susceptible to fire to OHV use during the fire season.

2. Quickly suppress fires that do occur
   a. Implement policy changes that allow access to more fire suppression resources, such as Air National Guard Mobile Airborne Firefighting Units.
   b. Re-allocate fire response resources (crews, equipment, etc.) to important sage-grouse habitats. Identify where resources are lacking and provide those resources to decrease response time to fires in sage-grouse habitats.
   c. Establish defensible fire lines in areas where: (i) effectiveness is high, (ii) fire risk is likely, and (iii) negative impacts from these efforts (e.g. fragmentation) are minimized. Avoid use of any vegetative stripping in healthy, unfragmented habitats, unless fire conditions and local ecological conditions so warrant.
   d. Carefully consider the use of backfires within PACs to minimize the potential for escape and further damage to sage-grouse and sagebrush habitats.
   e. Provide education of fire personnel on the need and value of protecting sagebrush landscapes.
   f. Remove pinyon-juniper stands which are highly flammable (stands where trees are the dominant vegetation and the primary plant influencing ecological processes (Phase 3; Miller *et al.* 2008)) in low elevation sagebrush habitats.
   g. Reduce risk of human-caused fires by limiting activities that may result in fire (e.g., fire bans for campers, limit OHV use to roads) during high risk fire seasons.
   h. Provide incentives for suppressing fires in sagebrush habitats.
   i. Federal land management agencies should consider placing additional firefighting resources and establish new Incident Attack Centers in or adjacent to PACs.
   j. Firefighters should ensure close coordination with firefighters from other management agencies and local fire departments. Additionally they should seek

local expertise to create the best possible strategies for responding to and suppressing wildfire.

3. Improve restoration support
    a. Consider re-allocation of funding from other habitat work to restoration of sage-grouse habitats affected by fire.
    b. Address shortage of locally-adapted seed and storage capabilities.
    c. Apply available seed where it is most likely to be effective and to areas of highest need.
    d. Ensure sage-grouse habitat needs are considered in restoration efforts including managing for the range of variation, as appropriate for the local area.
    e. In the case of limited resources, prioritize PACs over habitats outside of PACs for restoration efforts.

4. Renew and implement BLM Instructional Memorandum (IM) 2011-138 (Sage-grouse Conservation Related to Wildland Fire and Fuels Management; Bureau of Land Management 2011) until a decision is made on whether to incorporate the measures identified in the IM into Resource Management Plans.

Non-native, Invasive Plant Species

The increase in mean fire frequency has been facilitated by the incursion of nonnative annual grasses, primarily *Bromus tectorum* and *Taeniatherum asperum*, into sagebrush ecosystems (Billings 1994; Miller and Eddleman 2001). Exotic annual grasses and other invasive plants also alter habitat suitability for sage-grouse by reducing or eliminating native forbs and grasses essential for food and cover (75 FR 13910, and references therein). Annual grasses and noxious perennials continue to expand their range, facilitated by ground disturbances, including wildfire (Miller and Eddleman 2001), improper grazing (Young *et al.* 1972, 1976), agriculture (Benvenuti 2007), and infrastructure associated with energy development (Bergquist *et al.* 2007). Management of this threat is two-pronged: (1) control, or stopping the spread of invasive annual grasses, and (2) reduction or elimination of established invasive annual grasses. These activities should be prioritized in all sagebrush habitats, both within and outside of PACs because once established, invasive annual grasses are extremely difficult to control.

Conservation Objective: Maintain and restore healthy, native sagebrush plant communities.

Conservation Measures:

1. Retain all remaining large intact sagebrush patches, particularly at low elevations.
2. Reduce or eliminate disturbances that promote the spread of these invasive species, such as reducing fires to a "normal range" of fire activity for the local ecosystem, employing grazing management that maintains the perennial native grass and shrub community appropriate to the local site, reducing impacts from any source that allows for the

invasion by these species into undisturbed sagebrush habitats, and precluding the use of treatments intended to remove sagebrush.

3. Monitor and control invasive vegetation post-wildfire for at least three years.
4. Require best management practices for construction projects in and adjacent to sagebrush habitats to prevent invasion.
5. Restore altered ecosystems such that non-native invasive plants are reduced to levels that do not put the area at risk of conversion if a catastrophic event were to occur. This is especially important within Wyoming big sagebrush communities as these cover types are the most at risk to displacement by cheatgrass (Wisdom *et al.* 2005). While complete elimination of non-native invasive plants would be ideal, we acknowledge that this is unlikely given our current understanding of underlying ecological processes, shifts in climate, and lack of resources.

Energy Development

The increasing demand for renewable and non-renewable energy resources is resulting in continued development within the greater sage-grouse range, resulting in habitat loss, fragmentation, direct and indirect disturbance. Development results in sage-grouse population declines.

Conservation Objective: Energy development should be designed to ensure that it will not impinge upon stable or increasing sage-grouse population trends.

Addressing energy development and any subsequent successful restoration activities in sagebrush ecosystems will require consideration of local ecological conditions, which cannot be prescribed on a range-wide level. Where state sage-grouse management plans have already identified an effective strategy for energy development that meets the above objective, the strategies in those plans should be implemented. In all other situations, the following measures should be considered to avoid, reduce, or mitigate impacts from energy development.

Conservation Measures:

1. Avoid energy development in PACs (Doherty *et al.* 2010). Identify areas where leasing is not acceptable, or not acceptable without stipulations for surface occupancy that maintains sage-grouse habitats.
2. If avoidance is not possible within PACs due to pre-existing valid rights, adjacent development, or split estate issues, development should only occur in non-habitat areas, including all appurtenant structures, with an adequate buffer that is sufficient to preclude impacts to sage-grouse habitat from noise, and other human activities.
3. If development must occur in sage-grouse habitats due to existing rights and lack of reasonable alternative avoidance measures, the development should occur in the least suitable habitat for sage-grouse and be designed to ensure at a minimum that there are

no detectable declines in sage-grouse population trends (and seek increases if possible) by implementing the following:

a. Reduce and maintain the density of energy structures below which there are not impacts to the function of the sage-grouse habitats (as measured by no declines in sage-grouse use), or do not result in declines in sage-grouse populations within PACs.

b. Design development outside PACs to maintain populations within adjacent PACs and allow for connectivity among PACs.

c. Consolidate structures and infrastructure associated with energy development.

d. Reclamation of disturbance resulting from a proposed project should only be considered as mitigation for those impacts, not portrayed as minimization.

e. Design development to minimize tall structures (turbines, powerlines), or other features associated with the development (e.g., noise from drilling or ongoing operations; Blickley *et al.* 2012).

Sagebrush Removal

The intentional removal or treatment of sagebrush (using prescribed fire, or any mechanical and chemical tools to remove or alter the successional status of the sagebrush ecosystem) contributes to habitat loss and fragmentation, a primary factor in the decline of sage-grouse populations. Removal and manipulation of sagebrush may also increase the opportunities for the incursion of invasive annual grasses, particularly if the soil crust is disturbed (Beck *et al.* 2012). Although many treatments are often presented as improving sage-grouse habitats, data supporting the positive impacts of sagebrush manipulation on sage-grouse populations is limited (Beck *et al.* 2012).

Conservation Objective: Avoid sagebrush removal or manipulation in sage-grouse breeding or wintering habitats.

Exceptions to this can be considered where minor habitat losses are sustained while implementing other habitat improvement or maintenance efforts (e.g., juniper removal) and in areas used as late summer brood habitat (Connelly *et al.* 2000). Appropriate regulatory and incentive-based mechanisms must be implemented to preclude sagebrush removal and manipulation for all other purposes.

Grazing

Livestock grazing is the most widespread type of land use across the sagebrush biome (Connelly *et al.* 2004) and almost all sagebrush areas are managed for livestock grazing (Knick *et al.* 2003). Improper livestock management, as determined by local ecological conditions, may have negative impacts on sage-grouse seasonal habitats (75 FR 13910 and references therein), and management to enhance populations of wild ungulates may also have negative impacts (e.g. removal of sagebrush overstory in an attempt to increase forage production for wild ungulates).

Conservation Objective: Conduct grazing management for all ungulates in a manner consistent with local ecological conditions that maintains or restores healthy sagebrush shrub and native perennial grass and forb communities and conserves the essential habitat components for sage-grouse (e.g. shrub cover, nesting cover). Areas which do not currently meet this standard should be managed to restore these components. Adequate monitoring of grazing strategies and their results, with necessary changes in strategies, is essential to ensuring that desired ecological conditions and sage-grouse response are achieved.

Achieving the above objective will require the development of long-term strategies that provide seasonal habitats for sage-grouse. Although grazing management should initially focus on retaining the above habitat conditions within PACs, sound grazing management should be applied across all sagebrush habitats. Grazing management strategies must consider the local ecological conditions, including soil types, precipitation zones, vegetation composition and drought conditions. Livestock and wild ungulate numbers must be managed at levels that allow native sagebrush vegetative communities to minimally achieve Proper Functioning Conditions (PFC; for riparian areas) or Rangeland Health Standards (RHS; uplands). Similar measures should be implemented on non-federal land surfaces.

There are several potentially useful tools for developing management strategies (such as Ecological Site Descriptions (ESDs) and PFC metrics. However, use of these tools must be tied to sage-grouse habitat and population parameters if they are to be considered as a sole measure for monitoring condition and, if appropriate, rehabilitation progress (Doherty *et al*. 2011). ESDs are not available across the entire range. Given the utility of ESDs in developing local management strategies, ESDs should be completed throughout the entire range of sage-grouse.

Implementation of the following options could help reduce any threats that grazing may pose to sage-grouse.

Conservation Options:

1. Ensure that allotments meet ecological potential and wildlife habitat requirements; and, ensure that the health and diversity of the native perennial grass community is consistent with the ecological site.
2. Inform and educate affected grazing permittees regarding sage-grouse habitat needs and conservation measures.
3. Incorporate sage-grouse habitat needs or habitat characteristics into relevant resource and allotment management plans, including the desired conditions with the understanding that these desired conditions may not be fully achievable: (a) due to the existing ecological condition, ecological potential or the existing vegetation; or (b) due to causal events unrelated to existing livestock grazing.
4. Conduct habitat assessments and, where necessary, determine factors causing any failure to achieve the habitat characteristics. Make adjustments as appropriate.

5. Given limited agency resources, priority should be given to PACs and then sage-grouse habitats adjacent to PACs.

Range Management Structures

Structures which support range management activities can have negative impacts on sage-grouse habitats by increasing fragmentation (e.g., fences and roads) or diminishing habitat quality (e.g., concentrating ungulates in winter habitats). Typical range management structures include fences, water developments and mineral licks. As fences can be both a positive and negative impact on sage-grouse and their habitats, depending on their location and use, they are addressed in a separate section below.

Conservation Objective: Avoid or reduce the impact of range management structures on sage-grouse.

Conservation Measures:

1. Range management structures should be designed and placed to be neutral or beneficial to sage-grouse.
2. Structures that are currently contributing to negative impacts to either sage-grouse or their habitats should be removed or modified to remove the threat.

Free-Roaming Equid Management

Free-roaming equid grazing is presented separately from ungulate grazing due to the differing impacts equids have on sagebrush ecosystems. On a per capita body mass, horses consume more forage than cattle or sheep and remove more of the plant which limits and/or delays vegetative recovery (Menard *et al.* 2002), and horses can range further between water sources than cattle, thereby making them more difficult to manage. Equid grazing results in a reduction of shrub cover and more fragmented shrub canopies, which can negatively affect sage-grouse habitat (Beever and Aldridge 2011). Additionally, sites grazed by free-roaming equids have a greater abundance of annual invasive grasses, reduced native plant diversity and reduced grass density (Beever and Aldridge 2011). Given the high mobility of free-roaming equids, the conservation measures below should be applied across all sage-grouse habitats.

Conservation Objective: Protect sage-grouse from the negative influences of grazing by free-roaming equids.

Conservation Measures

1. Develop, implement, and enforce adequate regulatory mechanisms to protect sage-grouse habitat from negative influences of grazing by free-roaming equids.

2. Manage free-roaming equids at levels that allow native sagebrush vegetative communities to minimally achieve PFC (for riparian areas) or RHS (for uplands). Similar measures should be implemented on non-federal land surfaces.

Conservation Options
1. Determine if the current appropriate management levels (AMLs) maintain suitable sage-grouse habitat parameters. Support additional research to quantitatively determine impacts of wild horses and burros on sage-grouse habitat parameters.
2. Until research on AMLs is completed, manage for AMLs within horse management areas on federal lands. Current AMLs should be adjusted for drought conditions.
3. Develop scientific procedures that can be replicated to count horses so that proper management actions can be implemented when numbers exceed AMLs.
4. Develop a sound monitoring program with prescriptive management "triggers" to make adjustments in horse and burro numbers or their distribution, as necessary.

Pinyon-juniper Expansion

Greater sage-grouse are negatively impacted by the expansion of pinyon and/or juniper in their habitats, even if the underlying sagebrush habitats remain (Freese *et al.* 2009). Sage-grouse avoid these areas of expansion (Casazza *et al.* 2010), and as the pinyon and/or juniper increases in abundance and size, the underlying habitat quality for sage-grouse diminishes.

Conservation Objective: Remove pinyon-juniper from areas of sagebrush that are most likely to support sage-grouse (post-removal) at a rate that is at least equal to the rate of pinyon-juniper incursion.

Treatments to remove pinyon and/or juniper trees in phase 1 (trees present but shrubs and herbs are the dominant vegetation that influence ecological processes) and phase 2 (tress are co-dominant with shrubs and herbs and all three vegetation layers influence ecological processes; Miller *et al.* 2008) state of incursion should match the rate of incursion (minimally 200,000 acres per year; Stiver *et al.* 2006). Removal should be prioritized by seasonal habitats, based on the habitat that is locally limiting populations. Removal techniques should not include prescribed fire in low elevation, xeric sagebrush communities.

Pinyon and/or juniper removal activities should focus initially on areas within PACs, but all opportunities to remove this threat should be considered if resources are available. Where state sage-grouse management plans provide an effective strategy for pinyon-juniper, those strategies should be implemented. In all other situations the following conservation options should be considered.

Conservation Options:

1. Prioritize the use of mechanical treatments for removing pinyon and/or juniper. These techniques allow for more selective removal of invading plants, and more importantly allows understory habitats to remain intact.
2. Use caution when planning use of prescribed fire in high elevation mountain big sage sites to prevent fire escape and any subsequent establishment of invasive annual grasses or other weeds.
3. Reduce juniper cover in sage-grouse habitats to less than 5% (Freese 2009, Cassaza *et al.* 2010), but preferably eliminate entirely.
4. Employ all necessary management actions to maintain the benefit of pinyon and/or juniper removal for sage-grouse habitats, including long-term monitoring (greater than 30 years) with appropriate management responses should the resultant habitat quality decline.

Agricultural Conversion

Agricultural conversion is typically defined as the conversion of sagebrush habitats to tilled agricultural crops or re-seeded exotic grass pastures, resulting in habitat loss and fragmentation. Agricultural conversion can also be the conversion of conservation (e.g., those enrolled in the Conservation Reserve Program (CRP) or State Acres for Wildlife Enhancement (SAFE)) when such lands are providing important habitat components for sage-grouse. This type of conversion could be detrimental to sage-grouse in areas where the birds depend on these interim successional habitats (such as in Washington).

Conservation Objective: Avoid further loss of sagebrush habitat for agricultural activities (both plant and animal production) and prioritize restoration. In areas where taking agricultural lands out of production has benefited sage-grouse, the programs supporting these actions should be targeted and continued (e.g. CRP/SAFE). Threat amelioration activities should, at a minimum, be prioritized within PACs, but should be considered in all sage-grouse habitats.

Conservation Options:

1. Revise Farm Bill policies and commodity programs that facilitate ongoing conversion of native habitats to marginal croplands (e.g., through the addition of a 'Sodsaver' provision), to support conservation of remaining sagebrush-steppe habitats.
2. Continue and expand incentive programs that encourage the maintenance of sagebrush habitats.
3. Develop criteria for set-aside programs which stop negative habitat impacts and promote the quality and quantity sage-grouse habitat.
4. If lands that provide seasonal habitats for sage-grouse are taken out of a voluntary program, such as CRP or SAFE, precautions should be taken to ensure withdrawal of the lands minimizes the risk of direct take of sage-grouse (e.g., timing to avoid

nesting season). Voluntary incentives should be implemented to increase the amount of sage-grouse habitats enrolled in these programs.

Mining

Surface mining and appurtenant facilities within sage-grouse habitats result in the direct loss of habitat, habitat fragmentation, and indirect impacts from disturbance (e.g., noise, dust). Current reclamation activities do not always consider sage-grouse habitat needs. Those that do may take decades to restore habitats and experience the same limitations as restoration activities. Surface facilities supporting underground mining activities can have similar impacts.

Conservation Objective: Maintain stable to increasing sage-grouse populations and no net loss of sage-grouse habitats in areas affected by mining.

Reclamation of mined lands within sage-grouse habitats should be focused on restoring habitats usable by sage-grouse, and the re-establishment of sage-grouse in these areas. Where state sage-grouse management plans provide effective conservation strategies for mining those strategies should be implemented. In all other situations the following conservation options should be considered.

Conservation Options:
1. Avoid new mining activities and/or any associated facilities within occupied habitats, including seasonal habitats;
2. Avoid leasing in sage-grouse habitats until other suitable habitats can be restored to habitats used by sage-grouse;
3. Reclamation plans should focus on restoring areas disturbed by mining and associated facilities to healthy sagebrush ecosystems, including evidence of use by sage-grouse.
4. Reclamation of abandoned mine lands should focus on restoring areas to healthy sagebrush ecosystems where possible.

Recreation

Recreational activities within sage-grouse habitats can result in habitat loss and fragmentation (e.g., creation of off-road trails, camping facilities) and both direct and indirect disturbance to the birds (e.g., noise, disruptive lek viewing, hunting dog trials, and dispersed camping).

Conservation Objective: In areas subjected to recreational activities, maintain healthy native sagebrush communities based on local ecological conditions and with consideration of drought conditions, and manage direct and indirect human disturbance (including noise) to avoid interruption of normal sage-grouse behavior.

Threat amelioration for recreation should be implemented in PACs, but considered in all sage-grouse habitats. Where state sage-grouse management plans provide an effective strategy for recreational activities, those strategies should be implemented. In all other situations the following conservation options should be considered.

Conservation Options:

1. Close important sage-grouse use areas to off-road vehicle use.
2. Avoid development of recreational facilities (e.g., new roads and trails, campgrounds) in sage-grouse habitats.

Ex-Urban Development

Ex-urban development (dispersed homes on small acreages) results in direct habitat loss, habitat fragmentation, and the introduction of invasive plant species. Urban and exurban activities also increase the presence of predator subsidies (e.g., trash, landfills, bird feeders) allowing for increased predators associated with humans that may have disproportionate impacts on greater sage-grouse (e.g., red fox, skunks, raccoons). Additionally, pets may have negative impacts on sage-grouse through direct predation or disturbance (e.g., chasing birds). Infrastructure associated with exurban development (e.g., powerlines, roads) also results in habitat loss and fragmentation, subsidies for avian predators such as ravens, and possible disturbance to sage-grouse. Moreover, concentration of hobby livestock on small acreages can result in habitat loss and the introduction of invasive annual grasses and weeds.

Conservation Objective: Limit urban and exurban development in sage-grouse habitats and maintain intact native sagebrush plant communities.

At a minimum, threat amelioration for ex-urban development should occur within PACs, but should also be considered in all sage-grouse habitats. Where state sage-grouse management plans provide an effective strategy for managing ex-urban development, they should be implemented. In all other situations the following conservation options should be considered.

Conservation Options:

1. Provide incentives to maintaining large tracts of private lands that provide habitat for sage-grouse. These incentives can include (but may not be limited to):
    a. Developing habitat conservation plans;
    b. Conservation easements or leases; and/or
    c. Land swaps.
2. Acquire and manage sage-grouse habitat to maintain intact ecosystems.
3. Consolidate infrastructure that supports urban and exurban development.
4. Do not allow landfills in sage-grouse habitats, or within 5 km of sage-grouse habitats.

5. Do not relinquish public lands for the purpose of urban development in sage-grouse habitat.

Infrastructure

Development of infrastructure for any purpose (e.g., roads, pipelines, powerlines, and cellular towers) results in habitat loss, fragmentation, and may cause sage-grouse habitat avoidance. Additionally, infrastructure can provide sources for the introduction of invasive plant species and predators.

Conservation Objective: Avoid development of infrastructure within PACs.

Conservation Measures:

There should be no new development of infrastructure corridors within PACs. Designated, but not yet developed infrastructure corridors should be re-located outside of PACs unless it can be demonstrated that these corridors will have no impacts on the maintenance of neutral or positive sage-grouse population trends and habitats. New infrastructure should be avoided where individual state plans have identified key connectivity corridors outside of PACs.

Where state sage-grouse management plans provide an effective strategy for infrastructure those strategies should be implemented. In all other situations the following conservation options should be considered.

Conservation Options:

1. Avoid construction of these features in sage-grouse habitat, both within and outside of PACs.
2. Power transmission corridors which cannot avoid PACs should be buried (if technically feasible) and disturbed habitat should be restored.
   a. If avoidance is not possible, consolidate new structures with existing features and/or preclude development of new structures within locally important sage-grouse habitats.
      i. Consolidation with existing features should not result in a cumulative corridor width of greater than 200m.
      ii. Habitat function lost from placement of infrastructure should be replaced.
3. Infrastructure corridors should be designed and maintained to preclude introduction of invasive plant species.
4. Restrictions limiting use of roads should be enforced.
5. Remove transmission lines and roads that are duplicative or are not functional.

6. Transmission line towers should be constructed to severely reduce or eliminate nesting and perching by avian predators, most notably ravens, thereby reducing anthropogenic subsidies to those species.
7. Avoid installation of compressor stations in PACs or other sage-grouse habitats where sage-grouse would be affected by noise and operation activities.
8. All commercial pipelines should be buried and habitat that is disturbed needs to be reclaimed with current and future emphasis placed on suppression of non-native invasive plant species.
9. Mitigate impacts to habitat from development of these features.
10. Remove (or decommission) non-designated roads within sagebrush habitats.

Fences

Fences can be deleterious to sage-grouse populations and habitats, with threats including habitat fragmentation and direct mortality through strikes (Stevens *et al.* 2012). Fences can improve habitat conditions for sage-grouse (e.g. by protecting riparian areas providing brood-rearing habitats from overgrazing). The assessment of the impact or benefit of fences must be made considering local ecological conditions and the movement of sage-grouse within local areas (Stevens *et al.* 2012).

Conservation Objective: Minimize the impact of fences on sage-grouse populations.

Conservation Options:

1. Mark fences that are in high risk areas for collision (Stevens *et al.* 2012) with permanent flagging or other suitable device to reduce sage-grouse collisions on flat to gently rolling terrain in areas of moderate to high fence densities (i.e., more than 1 km of fence per km^2) located within 2 kms of occupied leks.
2. Identify and remove unnecessary fences.
3. Placement of new fences and livestock management facilities (including corrals, loading facilities, water tanks and windmills) should consider their impact on sage-grouse and, to the extent practicable, be placed at least 1 km from occupied leks (Stevens *et al.* 2012).

6. LITERATURE CITED

75 FR 13910. 2010. U.S. Fish and Wildlife Service. Endangered and threatened wildlife and Plants; 12-month finding for petitions to list the greater sage-grouse as threatened or endangered; proposed rule. 106pp.

Aldridge, C.L. and M.S. Boyce. 2007. Linking occurrence and fitness to persistence: a habitat-based approach for endangered greater sage-grouse. Ecological Applications 17:508-526.

Aldridge, C.L. and R.M. Brigham. 2003. Distribution, abundance, and status of the greater sage-grouse, *Centrocercus urophasianus*, in Canada. Canadian Field-Naturalist 117:25-34.

Aldridge, C.L., S.E. Nielsen, H.L. Beyer, M.S. Boyce, J.W. Connelly, S.T. Knick, and M.A. Schroeder. 2008. Range-wide patterns of greater sage-grouse persistence. Diversity and Distributions 14:983–994.

Archer, S., D.S. Schimel, and E.A. Holland. 1995. Mechanisms of shrubland expansion: land use, climate or CO_2. Climate Change 29:91-99

Baker, W.L. 2011. Pre-EuroAmerican and recent fire in sagebrush ecosystems. Pp. 185-202 *in* S.T. Knick and J.W. Connelly (eds). Greater Sage-Grouse: ecology and conservation of a landscape species and its habitats. Studies in Avian Biology (vol. 38). University of California Press, Berkeley, CA.

Balch, J.K., B.A. Bradley, C.M. D'Antonio and J.Gomez-Dans. 2013. Introduced annual grass increases regional fire activity across the arid western USA (1980 – 2009). Global Change Biology 19:173-183.

Barnett, J.K. and J.A. Crawford. 1994. Pre-laying nutrition of sage grouse hens in Oregon. Journal of Range Management 47:114-118.

Beck, J.L., D.L. Mitchell, and B.D. Maxfield. 2003. Changes in the distribution and status of sage-grouse in Utah. Western North American Naturalist 63:203-214.

Beck, J.L., J.W. Connelly, and C.L. Wambolt. 2012. Consequences of treating Wyoming big sagebrush to enhance wildlife habitats. Rangeland Ecol. Manage. 65:444-455.

Becker, J.M., C.A. Duberstein, J.D. Tagestad, and J.L. Downs. 2009. Sage-grouse and wind energy: biology, habits, and potential effects from development PNNL-18567. US Dept. of Energy. Pacific Northwest National Laboratory, Richland, WA.

Bedrosian B. and D. Craighead. 2010. Sage-grouse completion report: 2007 – 2009. Unpublished report, Craighead Beringia South, Kelly, WY. 119pp.

Beever, E.A. and C.L. Aldridge. 2011. Influences of free-roaming equids on sagebrush ecosystems, with focus on greater sage-grouse. Pp. 273-290 *in* S.T. Knick and J.W. Connelly (eds). Greater Sage-Grouse: ecology and conservation of a landscape species and its habitats. Studies in Avian Biology (vol. 38). University of California Press, Berkeley, CA.

Benedict, N.G., S.J. Oyler-McCance, S.E. Taylor, C.E. Braun, and T.W. Quinn. 2003. Evaluation of the eastern (*Centrocercus urophasianus urophasianus*) and western (*Centrocercus urophasianus phaios*) sub-species of sage-grouse using mitochondrial control-region sequence data. Conservation Genetics 4:301-310.

Benvenuti, S. 2007. Weed seed movement and dispersal strategies in the agricultural environment. Weed Biology and Management, 7:141-157.

Bergquist, E., P. Evangelista, T.J. Stohlgren, and N. Alley. 2007. Invasive species and coal bed methane development in the Powder River Basin, Wyoming. Environmental Monitoring and Assessment 128:381-394.

Berryman A.A. 2002. Population: a central concept for ecology? Oikos 97:439-442.

Billings, W.D. 1994. Ecological impacts of cheatgrass and resultant fire on ecosystems in the western Great Basin. Pp. 22-30 *in* Monsen, Stephen B.; Kitchen, Stanley G., comps. Proceedings--ecology and management of annual rangelands; 1992,,Boise ID, Gen. Tech. Rep. INT-GTR-313. Ogden, UT: U.S. Department of Agriculture, Forest Service, Intermountain Research Station.

Blank, R.R. and Morgan, T. 2012. Suppression of *Bromus tectorum* L. by Established Perennial Grasses: Potential Mechanisms—Part One. Applied and Environmental Soil Science. Volume 2012, Article ID 632172, 9pp.

Blickley, J.L., D. Blackwood and G.L. Patricelli. 2012. Experimental evidence for the effects of chronic anthropogenic noise on abundance of greater sage-grouse leks. Conservation Biology 26:461-471.

Blomberg, E. J., J.S. Sedinger, M.T. Atamian, and D.V. Nonne. 2012. Characteristics of climate and landscape disturbance influence the dynamics of greater sage-grouse populations. Ecosphere 3(6):55, 20pp.

Braun, C.E. 1998. Sage grouse declines in western North America: What are the problems? Proceedings of Western Association of Fish and Wildlife Agencies 78:139-156.

Braun, C.E., M.F. Baker, R.L. Eng, J.W. Gashwiler, and M.H. Schroeder. 1976. Conservation committee report on effects of alteration of sagebrush communities on the associated avifauna. Wilson Bulletin 88:165-171.

Bureau of Land Management. 2011. Instructional Memorandum 2011-138. Sage-grouse conservation related to wildland fire and fuels management. Bureau of Land Management, Washington D.C. 9pp.

Cassaza M.L., P.S. Coates, and C.T. Overton. 2010. Linking habitat selection to brood success in greater sage-grouse, Pp. 151-167 *in* B.K. Sandercock, K.Martin and G. Segelbacher (eds.). Ecology, conservation and management of grouse. Studies in Avian Biology (no. 39). University of California Press, Berkeley, CA.

CGSSC (Colorado Greater Sage-grouse Steering Committee). 2008. Colorado greater sage-grouse conservation plan. Colorado Division of Wildlife, Denver, CO.

Connelly, J.W. and C.E. Braun. 1997. Long-term changes in sage grouse *Centrocercus urophasianus* populations in western North America. Wildlife Biology 3:229-234.

Connelly, J.W., H.W. Browers, and R.J. Gates. 1988. Seasonal movements of sage grouse in southeastern Idaho. Journal of Wildlife Management 52:116-122.

Connelly, J.W., M.A. Schroeder, A.R. Sands, and C.E. Braun. 2000. Guidelines to manage sage grouse populations and their habitats. Wildlife Society Bulletin 28:967-985.

Connelly, J.W., S.T. Knick, M.A. Schroeder, and S.J. Stiver. 2004. Conservation assessment of greater sage-grouse and sagebrush habitats. Unpublished Report, Western Association of Fish and Wildlife Agencies. Cheyenne, WY. 610pp.

Connelly, J.W., C.A. Hagen, and M.A. Schroeder. 2011a. Characteristics and dynamics of greater sage-grouse populations. Pp. 53-68 *in* S.T. Knick and J.W. Connelly (eds). Greater Sage-Grouse: ecology and conservation of a landscape species and its habitats. Studies in Avian Biology (vol. 38). University of California Press, Berkeley, CA.

Connelly, J.W., E.T. Rinkes, and C.E. Braun. 2011b. Characteristics of greater sage-grouse habitats: a landscape species at micro and macro scales. Pp. 69-84 *in* S.T. Knick and J.W. Connelly (eds). Greater Sage-Grouse: ecology and conservation of a landscape species and its habitats. Studies in Avian Biology (vol. 38). University of California Press, Berkeley, CA.

CPW (Colorado Parks and Wildlife). 2008. Draft Implementation Plan for the Colorado Greater Sage-grouse Conservation Plan. Colorado Parks and Wildlife draft report developed with Federal and State Agencies and Local Working Groups.

CPW (Colorado Parks and Wildlife). 2012. Colorado Parks and Wildlife Greater Sage-Grouse Preliminary Priority and General in Colorado. Updated September 2012: http://wildlife.state.co.us/WildlifeSpecies/SpeciesOfConcern/Birds/Pages/GreaterSage-grousePriorityHabitat.aspx

Davis, D.M. 2012. Population structure of greater sage-grouse in northeastern California: Implications for conservation in a declining peripheral population. Ph.D. Dissertation. University of Idaho, December, 2012. 236pp.

Delong, A.K., J.A. Crawford, and D.C. Delong, Jr. 1995. Relationships between vegetational structure and predation of artificial sage grouse nests. Journal of Wildlife Management 59:88-92.

Doherty, K.E., D.E. Naugle, B.L. Walker, and J.M. Graham. 2008. Greater sage-grouse winter habitat selection and energy development. Journal of Wildlife Management 72:187-195.

Doherty, K.E., J.D. Tack, J.S. Evans, and D.E. Naugle. 2010. Mapping breeding densities of greater sage-grouse: A tool for range-wide conservation planning. BLM completion report: Agreement # L10PG00911. http://www.blm.gov/pgdata/etc/medialib/blm/wo/Communications_Directorate/public_aff airs.Par.46599.File.dat/GRSG%20Rangewide%20Breeding%20Density.pdf

Doherty, K.E., J.L. Beck, and D.E. Naugle. 2011. Comparing ecological site descriptions to habitat characteristics influencing Greater sage-grouse nest site occurrence and success. Rangeland Ecology and Management 64:344-351.

Dunn, P.O. and C.E. Braun. 1986. Late summer-spring movements of juvenile sage-grouse. Wilson Bulletin 98:83-92.

Fedy B.C., C.L. Aldridge, K.E Doherty, M. O'Donnell, J.L. Beck, B. Bedrosian, M.J. Holloran, G.D. Johnson, N.W. Kaczor, C.P. Kirol, C.A. Mandich, D. Marshall, G. McKee, C. Olson, C.C. Swanson, and B.L. Walker. 2012. Interseasonal movements of Greater sage-grouse, migratory behavior, and an assessment of the core regions concept in Wyoming. Journal of Wildlife Management 76:1062-1071.

Freese, M.T. 2009. Linking greater sage-grouse habitat use and suitability across spatiotemporal scales in central Oregon. M.S. Thesis, Oregon State University, Corvallis, OR. 123pp.

Garton, E.O., J.W. Connelly, J.S. Horne, C.A. Hagen, A. Moser, and M. Schroeder. 2011. Greater sage-grouse population dynamics and probability of persistence. Pp. 293-382 in S.T. Knick and J.W. Connelly (eds). Greater Sage-Grouse: ecology and conservation of a landscape species and its habitats. Studies in Avian Biology (vol. 38). University of California Press, Berkeley, CA.

Gregg, M.A. 1991. Use and selection of nesting habitat by sage grouse in Oregon. M.S. Thesis, Oregon State University, Corvallis, OR. 56pp.

Gregg, M.A., J.A. Crawford, M.S. Drut, and A.K. DeLong. 1994. Vegetational cover and predation of sage grouse nests in Oregon. Journal of Wildlife Management 58:162-166.

Hagen, C.A. 2010. Impacts of energy development on prairie grouse ecology: a research synthesis. Transactions of North American Wildlife and Natural Resource Conference 75:96-103.

Hagen, C.A. 2011a. Predation on sage-grouse: facts, effects, and process. Pp. 95-100 *in* S. T. Knick and J. W. Connelly. Greater Sage-Grouse: ecology and conservation of a landscape species and its habitat. Studies in Avian Biology 38. University of California Press, Berkeley, CA.

Hagen, C.A. 2011b. Greater sage-grouse conservation assessment and strategy for Oregon: A plan to maintain and enhance populations and habitats. Oregon Department of Fish and Wildlife, Bend, OR. 221pp.

Herman-Brunson, K.M. 2007. Nesting and brood-rearing habitat selection of greater sage-grouse and associated survival of hens and broods at the edge of their historic distribution. Thesis, South Dakota State University, Brookings, SD.

Holloran, M.J. 2005. Greater sage-grouse (*Centrocercus urophasianus*) population response to natural gas field development in western Wyoming. Ph.D Dissertation, University of Wyoming, Laramie, WY. 215pp.

Holloran, M.J. and S.H. Anderson. 2004. Greater sage-grouse seasonal habitat selection and survival in Jackson Hole, Wyoming. Job Completion Report, Wyoming Game and Fish Department, Cheyenne, WY.

Johnsgard, P.A. 2002. Grassland grouse and their conservation. Smithsonian Institution Press, Washington and London. 157pp.

Johnson, G.D. and M.S. Boyce. 1991. Survival, growth, and reproduction of captive reared sage grouse. Wildlife Society Bulletin 19:88-93.

Johnson, K.H. and C.E. Braun. 1999. Viability and conservation of an exploited sage-grouse population. Conservation Biology 13:77-84.

Kaiser, R.C. 2006. Recruitment by greater sage-grouse in association with natural gas development in western Wyoming. M.S. Thesis, University of Wyoming, Laramie, WY. 102pp.

Kiesecker J.M., H.E. Copeland, B.A. McKenney, A. Pocewicz and K.E. Doherty. 2011. Energy by design: Making mitigation work for conservation and development. Pp. 159-181 *in* D.E. Naugle (ed). Energy Development and Wildlife Conservation in Western North America. Island Press, Washington, D.C.

Klebenow, D.A. and G.M. Gray. 1968. Food habits of juvenile sage grouse. Journal of Range Management 21:80-83.

Knick, S.T. 2011. Historical development, principal federal legislation and current management of sagebrush habitats: implications for conservation. Pp. 13-32 *in* S.T. Knick and J.W. Connelly (eds). Greater Sage-Grouse: ecology and conservation of a landscape species and its habitats. Studies in Avian Biology (vol. 38). University of California Press, Berkeley, CA.

Knick, S.T. and S.E. Hanser. 2011. Connecting pattern and process in greater sage-grouse populations and sagebrush landscapes. Pp. 383-406 *in* S.T. Knick and J.W. Connelly (eds). Greater Sage-Grouse: ecology and conservation of a landscape species and its habitats. Studies in Avian Biology (vol. 38). University of California Press, Berkeley, CA.

Knick, S.T., D.S. Dobkin, J.T. Rotenberry, M.A. Schroeder, W.M. Vander Haegen, and C. Van Riper III. 2003. Teetering on the edge or too late? Conservation and research issues for avifauna of sagebrush habitats. Condor 105:611-634.

Knick, S.T., S.E. Hanser, R.F. Miller, D.A. Pyke, M.J. Wisdom, S.P. Finn, E.T. Rinkes, and C.J. Henny. 2011. Ecological influence and pathways of land use in sagebrush. Pp. 203-251 *in* S. T. Knick and J. W. Connelly. Greater Sage-Grouse: ecology and conservation of a landscape species and its habitat. Studies in Avian Biology (vol. 38). University of California Press, Berkeley, CA.

Knick, S.T. and J.W. Connelly. 2011. Greater sage-grouse and sagebrush: an introduction to the landscape. Pp. 1-9 *in* S.T. Knick and J.W. Connelly (eds). Greater Sage-Grouse: ecology and conservation of a landscape species and its habitats. Studies in Avian Biology (vol. 38). University of California Press, Berkeley, CA.

LeBeau, C.W. 2012. Evaluation of Greater sage-grouse reproductive habitat and response to wind energy development in south-central, Wyoming. M.S. Thesis, University of Wyoming, Laramie, WY. 138pp.

Leu, M. and S.E. Hanser. 2011. Influences of the human footprint on the sagebrush landscape patterns: implications for sage-grouse conservation. Pp. 253-272 *in* S.T. Knick and J.W. Connelly (eds). Greater Sage-Grouse: ecology and conservation of a landscape species and its habitats. Studies in Avian Biology (vol. 38). University of California Press, Berkeley, CA.

Lyon, A.G. 2000. The potential effects of natural gas development on sage grouse (*Centrocercus urophasianus*) near Pinedale, Wyoming. M.S. Thesis, University of Wyoming, Laramie, WY. 129pp.

Menard, C., P. Duncan, G. Fleurance, J-Y. Georges, and M. Lila. 2002. Comparative foraging and nutrition of horses and cattle in European wetlands. Journal of Applied Ecology 39:120-133.

Miller, R.F. and L.L. Eddleman. 2000. Spatial and temporal changes of sage grouse habitat in the sagebrush biome. Oregon State University Agricultural Experiment Station, Technical Bulletin 151. 37pp.

Miller, R.F. and L.L. Eddleman. 2001. Spatial and temporal changes of sage-grouse habitat in the sagebrush biome. Oregon State University Agricultural Experiment Station Technical Bulletin 151.

Miller, R.F. and J.A. Rose. 1999. Fire history and western juniper encroachment in sagebrush steppe. Journal of Range Management 52:550-559.

Miller, R.F. and R.J. Tausch. 2001. The role of fire in juniper and pinyon woodlands: a descriptive analysis. Pages 15-30 *In* Galley, K.E.M. and T.P. Wilson (eds). Proceedings of the invasive species workshop: The role of fire in the control and spread of invasive species. Fire Conference 2000: The First National Congress on Fire Ecology, Prevention, and Management. Miscellaneous Publication No. 11, Tall Timbers Research Station, Tallahassee, FL. 146pp.

Miller, R.F., Tausch, R.J., McArthur, E.D., D.D. Johnson and S.C. Sanderson. 2008. Age structure and expansion of piñon-juniper woodlands: a regional perspective in the Intermountain West. Research Paper Report RMRS-RP-69. Fort Collins, CO: U.S. Department of Agriculture, Forest Service, Rocky Mountain Research Station. 15pp.

Miller, R.F., S.T. Knick, D.A. Pyke, C.W. Meinke, S.E. Hanser, M.J. Wisdom, and A.L. Hild. 2011. Characteristics of sagebrush habitats and limitations to long-term conservation. Pp. 145-184 *in* S. T. Knick and J. W. Connelly (eds). Greater Sage-Grouse: ecology and conservation of a landscape species and its habitat. Studies in Avian Biology (vol. 38). University of California Press, Berkeley, CA.

Northeast Wyoming Sage-grouse Working Group. 2006. Northeast Wyoming Sage-grouse Conservation Plan. August 15, 2006. 177pp.

NWCOCP. 2008. Northwest Colorado greater sage-grouse conservation plan. Northwest Colorado Greater Sage-grouse Working Group, CO, USA.

Oyler-McCance, S.J., S.E. Taylor, and T.W. Quinn. 2005. A multilocus population genetic survey of Greater sage-grouse across their range. Molecular Ecology 14:1293-1310.

Patterson, R.L. 1952. The sage grouse in Wyoming. Wyoming Game and Fish Commission, Sage Books Inc., Denver, CO. 344pp.

Pedersen, E.K., J.W. Connelly, J.R. Hendrickson and W.E. Grant. 2003. Effect of sheep grazing and fire on sage grouse populations in southeastern Idaho. Ecological Modeling 165:23-47.

Pyke, D.A. 2011. Restoring and rehabilitating sagebrush habitats. Pp. 531-548 *in* S.T. Knick and J.W. Connelly (eds). Greater Sage-Grouse: ecology and conservation of a landscape species and its habitats. Studies in Avian Biology (vol. 38). University of California Press, Berkeley, CA.

Redford, K.H., G. Amoto, J. Baillie, P. Beldomenico, E.L. Bennett, N. Clum, R.Cook, G. Fonseca, S. Hedges, F. Launay, S. Lieberman, G.M. Mace, A. Murayama, A. Putnam, J.G. Robinson, H. Rosenbaum, E.W. Sanderson, S.N. Stuart, P. Thomas, and J. Thorbjarnarson. 2011. What does it mean to successfully conserve a (vertebrate) species? Bioscience 61:39-48.

Rowland, M.M., M. Leu, S.P. Finn, S. Hanser, L.H. Suring, J.M. Boys, C.W. Meinke, S.T. Knick, and M.J. Wisdom. 2005. Assessment of threats to sagebrush habitats and associated species of concern in the Wyoming Basins. Version 1, March 2005. Unpublished Report. USGS Biological Resources Discipline, Snake River Field Station, Boise, ID.

Schroeder, M.A. and R.K. Baydack. 2001. Predation and the management of prairie grouse. Wildlife Society Bulletin 29:24-32.

Schroeder, M.A., J.R. Young, and C.E. Braun. 1999. Sage grouse (*Centrocercus urophasianus*). 28 pages *In* Poole, A. and F. Gill, eds. The Birds of North America, No. 425. The Birds of North America, Inc., Philadelphia, PA.

Schroeder, M.A., C.L. Aldridge, A.D. Apa, J.R. Bohne, C.E. Braun, S.D. Bunnell, J.W. Connelly, P.A. Deibert, S.C. Gardner, M.A. Hilliard, G.D. Kobriger, S.M. McAdam, C.W. McCarthy, J.J. McCarthy, D.L. Mitchell, E.V. Rickerson, and S. J. Stiver. 2004. Distribution of sage-grouse in North America. Condor 106:363-376.

Schroeder, M.A., M. Atamian, H. Ferguson, M. Finch, K. Stonehouse, and D.W. Stinson. 2012. Re-introduction of greater sage-grouse to Lincoln County, Washington: Progress report. Washington Department of Fish and Wildlife, Olympia, WA.

Shaffer M.L. and B.A. Stein. 2010. Safeguarding our precious heritage. Pp. 301-321 *in* Stein, B.A., L. S. Kutner, and J.S. Adams (eds). Precious Heritage: The status of biodiversity in the United States. Oxford University Press, Oxford, NY.

Smith, R. 2013. Conserving Montana's sagebrush highway: long distance migration in sage-grouse. M.S. Thesis. University of Montana, Missoula, MT. 47pp.

Soulé, M.E. (ed). 1987. Viable populations for conservation. Cambridge University Press, Cambridge, UK.

Soulé, P.T. and P.A. Knapp. 1999. Western juniper expansion on adjacent disturbed and near-relict sites. Journal of Range Management 52:525-533.

Stevens, B.S., J.W. Connelly, and K.P. Reese. 2012. Multi-scale assessment of Grater sage-grouse fence collision as a function of site and broad scale factors. Journal of Wildlife Management 76:1370-1380.

Stinson, D.W., D.W. Hays, and M.A. Schroeder. 2004. Washington State Recovery Plan for the Greater Sage-Grouse. Washington Department of Fish and Wildlife, Olympia, WA. 109pp.

Stiver, S.J., A.D. Apa, J. Bohne, S.D. Bunnell, P.Deibert, S.Gardner, M. Hilliard, C. McCarthy, and M.A. Schroeder. 2006. Greater sage-grouse comprehensive conservation strategy. Unpublished Report, Western Association of Fish and Wildlife Agencies, Cheyenne, Wyoming. 444pp.

Swenson, J.E., C.A. Simmons, and C.D. Eustace. 1987. Decrease of sage grouse *Centrocercus urophasianus* after ploughing of sagebrush steppe. Biological Conservation 41:125-132.

Tack, J.D., D.E. Naugle, J.C. Carlson, and P.J. Fargey. 2011. Greater sage-grouse *Centrocercus urophasianus* migration links the USA and Canada: a biological basis for international prairie conservation. Oryx 46:64-68.

Taylor, R.T., D.E. Naugle, and L.S. Mills. 2012. Viability analysis for the conservation of sage-grouse populations: Buffalo Field Office, Wyoming. Final Report. 27 February 2012. Prepared for BLM. 46pp.

Thompson K.M., M.J. Holloran, S.J. Slater, J.L. Kuipers and S.H. Anderson. 2006. Early brood-rearing habitat use and productivity of Greater sage-grouse in Wyoming. Western North American Naturalist 66:332-342.

USFWS, (U.S. Fish and Wildlife Service). 2008. Sheldon National Wildlife Refuge Planning Update. Sheldon National Wildlife Refuge, NV. 9pp.

USFWS. (U. S. Fish and Wildlife Service). 2012. U.S. Fish and Wildlife Service land-based wind energy guidelines. *http://www.fws.gov/windenergy*

WAFWA (Western Association of Fish and Wildlife Agencies). 2008. Greater sage-grouse population trends: An analysis of lek count databases 1965-2007. Sage- and Columbian Sharp-tailed grouse Technical Committee, unpublished report. 126pp.

Walker, B.L. and D.E. Naugle. 2011. West Nile virus ecology in sagebrush habitat and impacts on greater sage-grouse populations. Pp. 127-144 *in* S.T. Knick and J.W. Connelly (eds). Greater Sage-Grouse: ecology and conservation of a landscape species and its habitats. Studies in Avian Biology (vol. 38). University of California Press, Berkeley, CA.

Walker, B.L., D.E. Naugle, and K.E. Doherty. 2007. Greater sage-grouse population response to energy development and habitat loss. Journal of Wildlife Management 71:2644-2654.

West, N.E. 1983. Chapters 11-16, Pp. 321-421 *in* West, N.E. (ed). Ecosystems of the world: temperate deserts and semi-deserts. Elsevier Scientific Publishing Company, New York, NY. 522pp.

West, N.E. and J.A. Young. 2000. Intermountain valleys and lower mountain slopes. Pp. 256-284 *in* Barbour, M.G. and W.D. Billings, eds. North American terrestrial vegetation, 2nd Edition. Cambridge University Press, Cambridge, UK. 708pp.

Wisdom, M.J., M.M Rowland, L.H. and Suring. 2005. Habitat Threats in the Sagebrush Ecosystem: Methods of Regional Assessment and Applications in the Great Basin. Alliance Communications Group, Lawrence, KS.

Wisdom, M.J., C.W. Meinke, S.T. Knick and M.A. Schroeder. 2011. Factors associated with extirpation of sage-grouse. Pp. 451-474 *in* S.T. Knick and J.W. Connelly (eds). Greater Sage-Grouse: ecology and conservation of a landscape species and its habitats. Studies in Avian Biology (vol. 38). University of California Press, Berkeley, CA.

Wyoming Executive Order 2010-4. 2010. Accessed July 31, 2012. *http://will.state.wy.us/sis/wydocs/execorders.html*

Wyoming Executive Order 2011-5. 2011. Accessed July 31, 2012. *http://governor.wy.gov/Documents/Sage Grouse Executive Order.pdf*

Young, J.A, R.A. Evans, and J. Major. 1972. Alien plants in the Great Basin. Journal of Range Management 25:194-201.

Young, J. A., R. A. Evans, and P.T. Tueller. 1976. Great Basin plant communities-pristine and grazed. Pp. 187-215 *in* R. Elston and P. Headrick (eds). Holocene environmental change in the Great Basin. Nevada Archaeological Survey, Research Paper 6, University of Nevada, Reno, NV.

APPENDIX A—MANAGEMENT ZONE AND POPULATION RISK ASSESSMENTS

See Figure 3 for a map of management zones and populations.

MANAGEMENT ZONE I: GREAT PLAINS

This management zone consists of four sage-grouse populations as identified by Garton *et al.* (2011), including the Dakotas, Northern Montana, Powder River Basin, and Yellowstone Watershed populations. All of these populations cross state or provincial boundaries. Garton *et al.* (2011) predicted an 11.1 percent chance this Management Zone will fall below 200 males by 2037, and a 24.0 percent chance it would fall below 200 males by 2107. Privately-owned lands are a major constituent of sagebrush landscapes in the Great Plains (66 percent), followed by BLM (17 percent), and then other ownerships (Knick 2011). After Management Zones II and IV, this zone contains some of the most connected networks of sage-grouse leks in the range (Knick and Hanser 2011). On the other hand, sagebrush habitat in 37 percent of this zone is 75-100 percent similar to sagebrush habitat in areas where extirpation has occurred (Wisdom *et al.* 2011). Generally, areas in this zone that are least similar to extirpated parts of the range include the western portions of Northern Montana and Powder River populations and the southeast corner of the Yellowstone Watershed population (Wisdom *et al.* 2011, Figure 18.5).

Dakotas

The Dakotas's population occurs on the far eastern edge of the range of sage-grouse. Much of the population occurs in the Cedar Creek Anticline. Garton *et al.* (2011) reported the minimum male count for this population at 587 and predicted a 66 percent chance that this population would dip below 200 males in the next 100 years. Population counts in 2012 for North and South Dakota were approximately 300, so this population as a whole very likely still exceeds 500 birds. Priority areas for conservation (PACs) in North and South Dakota are connected by general habitat consisting of limited sagebrush habitat. Sage-grouse movements generally occur east and west between the Dakotas's population and Montana. Connectivity between the sub-populations occurs through Montana's portion of the population (Knick and Hanser 2011). This area was identified as a PAC in Montana due to historically high density of sage-grouse and for the seasonal habitat it provides for birds from North Dakota, a likely conduit for genetic connectivity. The area is heavily influenced by oil and gas development and conversion of native rangeland to cropland is a major threat to the persistence of this sage-grouse population. Over-grazing in localized areas has degraded the sagebrush habitat and can reduce nesting success. Nesting success was positively correlated to grass cover in North Dakota (Herman-Brunson 2007). Overall, this population is small and at high risk.

Northern Montana

The Northern Montana Population is predominantly in northeast Montana but extends north into southern Saskatchewan and Alberta, making up these provinces' entire sage-grouse populations. Garton *et al*. (2011) reported a minimum male count for this population at over 2,700 males and projected a very low probability (i.e., two percent) of the population dipping below 200 males in the next 100 years. The southern portion of this area, south of the Milk River, has a high abundance of sage-grouse, has been designated as a PAC, and is predominately comprised of public land. Land use in this area is livestock grazing with limited dryland farming and irrigated hay production adjacent to creeks and rivers. In general, habitat in this PAC is expansive and intact and faces few if any significant threats, particularly on public lands. Grouse in this PAC make up the majority of birds in this population. North of the Milk River, habitats comprise a relatively low density of silver sagebrush and a correspondingly low density of sage-grouse. The sage-grouse habitats in this area include more private lands and, in some portions of this area, have a long history of grain farming and low to moderate densities of natural gas production. A PAC was designated in northern Valley County where relatively intact habitats provide for resident grouse as well as a conduit for spring and fall migrating sage-grouse between Saskatchewan and southern Valley County. This PAC is adjacent to considerable farming to the east but is itself relatively stable and lacks significant threats. One or more large conservation easements are in place to protect habitat values on key private lands in northern Valley County. Given the extent and limited threats associated with this population, it is considered to be at low risk.

Powder River Basin

The Powder River Basin occurs mostly in Northeast Wyoming, but an area in southern Montana comprises the extreme northern tip of this population. A recent sagebrush cover assessment estimated average cover of sagebrush in the Powder River Basin to be 35 percent, with an average sagebrush patch size less than 300 acres (Rowland *et al*. 2005). Sagebrush patch size in the Powder River Basin has decreased by more than 63 percent in 40 years, down from 820 acre patches and an overall coverage of 41 percent in 1964. Most of the occupied sage-grouse habitat in northeast Wyoming is privately owned. Approximately 70 percent of known leks are found on private land; the remaining 30 percent are found on FS, BLM, and state lands (Northeast Wyoming Sage-grouse Working Group 2006).

Garton *et al*. (2011) reported a minimum male count for this population at 3,042 and projected a high probability (86.2 percent) of falling below 200 males by 2107. A recent viability study done for BLM (Taylor *et al*. 2012) indicates that sage-grouse viability in the Powder River Basin is being impacted by multiple stressors including West Nile virus and energy development. Their results suggest that if development continues, future viability of the already small sage-grouse populations in northeast Wyoming will be compromised. The Powder River Basin holds vast energy resources including oil, natural gas, and coal bed natural gas (Northeast Wyoming Sage-grouse Working Group 2006). The state has a core area management strategy to help balance the priorities of retaining healthy sage-grouse population on the landscape and energy development.

Although the Montana piece of the Powder River Basin makes up a relatively small portion of the population, it may provide genetic connectivity with other Montana populations. Land use in Montana's portion of this population includes a mix of livestock grazing, coal mining, and shallow coal bed natural gas production. Montana identified relatively small but intact habitats that have limited energy development and may serve as remnant habitat for supporting small numbers of sage-grouse into the future. The expanding threat of energy development across the Powder River Basin and corresponding downward population index trend makes this overall an at-risk population.

Yellowstone Watershed

The Yellowstone Watershed Population is a large population covering an expansive area south of the Missouri River, making up the majority of sage-grouse habitats in southeast and south central Montana. Garton *et al.* (2011) reported a minimum male count of over 2,900 males. They further projected a 60 percent chance of this population dipping below 200 males in the next 100 years. Landownership is predominantly private with scattered tracts and blocks of public land. Livestock grazing and small grain farming are common in this area. Oil and gas developments are scattered across portions of this area. Extensive private lands have the potential for conversion of additional sagebrush habitats to farming and various forms of sagebrush eradication. Cropland conversion continues to take place in this area. Priority areas for conservation have been identified both in the western and southeastern portions of this population, where sage-grouse densities are greatest and habitats remain relatively intact. The western and southeastern PACs are separated by about 70 miles of a mix of habitats, including an interstate highway, the Yellowstone river corridor, and a patchwork of cropland intermingled with occupied sage-grouse habitat. Some portion of this space between PACs may be identified as a PAC in the future as movement corridors and habitats needed for population connectivity become better understood and defined. Overall this population is only potentially at-risk.

MANAGEMENT ZONE II: WYOMING BASIN

This management zone is made up of five sage-grouse populations as identified by Garton *et al.* (2011), including Jackson Hole, Laramie, Eagle-South Routt, Middle Park, and the Wyoming Basin. Colorado and Utah's portions of the Wyoming Basin are described separately as the NWCO and North Park subpopulations in Colorado, and the Rich-Summit-Morgan and Uintah Management Areas in Utah. This management zone represents the highest abundance of sage-grouse relative to other management zones across the sage-grouse's range. Garton *et al.* (2011) predicted a small, 0.3 percent chance, that this zone will fall below 200 males by 2037, and a 16.2 percent chance it would fall below 200 males by 2107. The majority of this management zone is represented by the Wyoming Basin population. Montana's portion of the zone is very small, only including the northern tip of the Wyoming Basin population in a portion of Carbon

County. BLM and privately-owned lands are major constituents of sagebrush landscapes in this zone, representing 49 percent and 35 percent of the ownership, respectively (Knick 2011). Management Zone II contains the most highly connected network of sage-grouse leks in the range (Knick and Hanser 2011). This zone is also a stronghold for sage-grouse because it contains the second largest area of habitat range-wide (and the largest in the eastern range) with low similarity to extirpated portions of the range (Wisdom *et al.* 2011).

The Colorado portion of this management zone appears to capture redundancy and representation in the PACs. Priority areas for conservation represent 61 percent of the occupied range in Colorado and 84 percent of the breeding birds in the state (CPW 2012). Being on the edge of the species' range, the Colorado populations within this management zone are somewhat isolated. Linkage zones have been mapped among the Colorado populations and subpopulations (i.e., Eagle-South Routt, Middle Park, North Park, and NWCO) (CPW 2012). It is assumed the habitat linkages will allow for movement between populations and will decrease the probability of extinction of the subpopulations by stabilizing population dynamics. Connectivity between Wyoming's and Colorado's PACs may be adequate in most areas, but there may be some areas to address in the northwest Colorado area.

Eagle-South Routt

This population occurs in north-central Colorado and is separated from nearby populations by distance and mountainous terrain (Garton *et al.* 2011). The Eagle-South Routt population adds to representation and redundancy within Management Zone II because of its location on the landscape and limited connectivity to other populations within this zone. Priority areas for conservation capture 68 percent of the occupied range in this population and include 100 percent of all known active leks. These areas also contain all habitats that were modeled "high probability of use" within four miles of leks that have been active in the last 10 years (CPW 2012). Redundancy is not captured within this population because it is a fairly isolated population that is also fairly small (the three year average number of males from 2010-2012 is 108). Populations (in terms of males only) in the late 1960s were likely in the high 200s (CGSSC 2008). The greatest threat to this population is loss of habitat from subdivision and housing development as well as the associated infrastructure and roads (CPW 2008; NWCOCP 2008). Pinyon-juniper encroachment has been, and continues to be, a significant threat to the population as well. This population is high risk because, given its smaller population size and isolation, a stochastic event could greatly negatively affect this population.

Middle Park

The Middle Park population occurs east of Eagle-South Routt in north-central Colorado and is separated from adjacent populations by distance and mountainous terrain (Garton *et al.* 2011). Representation and redundancy appear to be captured adequately in Middle Park. Priority areas for conservation capture 79 percent of the occupied range in this population and also include 95 percent of all known active leks. Furthermore, PACs contain 95 percent of all habitats that were modeled "high probability of use." Redundancy is captured reasonably well within this population because, although it currently has a three-year running average of 210 males, the

PACs include most of the known distribution of birds. Connectivity to the North Park population has been documented. Housing development is the most current and foreseeable threat. Grand County has experienced a high rate of human population growth in recent years. This high human population growth rate is projected to continue primarily due to its' proximity to major ski resorts and summer recreational activities. Although this is a relatively small sage-grouse population, Colorado Parks and Wildlife (CPW) does not believe the population has ever been very large. Since the 1970's, the population counts have been roughly between 200 and 325 males. Connectivity to the North Park population has always been somewhat naturally limited over Muddy Pass although CPW has documented birds moving over the pass. Overall this population is considered at-risk.

Laramie

This population consists of five leks located southwest of Laramie, Wyoming. Few birds are seen on these leks although one is routinely occupied by a small number of birds, despite the fact that the running average of the number of males per lek was zero from 2004 to 2007 (WAFWA 2008). None of these leks are contained in a PCA and four of these leks are threatened by proposed wind energy development. Overall this population is considered high risk.

Jackson Hole

The Jackson Hole population is a small population located near Jackson Hole, Wyoming. This population is geographically isolated due to surrounding topography and limited habitat. This population consists of 16 leks (13 active and three inactive in past 10 years), of which only one is considered large (averaging over 40 birds). Population trend information indicates that this population is decreasing slightly, declining from an average of 20.5 males per active lek in 2005 to 14.9 males per active lek in 2011. Most of the breeding habitat in this population is contained within a single PAC. However there are three small subpopulations that are isolated from the main Jackson Hole PAC: Gros Ventre (two leks); Star Valley/State Line (two leks in Idaho) and Hoback Basin (one lek). Threats to this population consist of internal habitat fragmentation resulting from wildfires, prescribed burns, herbivory of sagebrush by elk and bison winter feeding operations, urban development, and recreational activities. Grand Teton National Park and the National Elk Refuge encompass most of the PACs and protect much of the crucial habitat. This population exists in high mountain valleys with deep snowpack and the amount of available winter habitat is a limiting factor based on studies by Holloran and Anderson (2004) and Bedrosian and Craighead (2010). Yellowstone National Park is just to the north, making Jackson Hole a popular tourist destination. Skiing and snowmobiling are prime recreational activities during winter. Urban development is limited as a result of limited private lands within this population, but includes some crucial winter habitat. Recently, energy development has begun in the southern edge of this population (Hoback Basin). Population estimates, based on male lek counts, indicate that total population numbers fluctuate, with a high of approximately 500 birds. Modeled population forecasts suggest that populations will decline, and long-term persistence is unlikely (Garton *et al.* 2011). Due to low population numbers, population isolation and a high degree of threats, this population is considered high risk.

Wyoming Basin

This large population extends into Montana, Idaho, Utah, and Colorado. The population is separated from adjacent populations by distance and topography (Garton *et al*. 2011). This population is the largest population within the species' range (> 20,000 males attending leks annually), and is very robust. However, long-term population trends are slightly downward, although recent counts suggest an increase. Even so, population modeling suggests that declines will continue over the long-term (Garton *et al*. 2011). This population is described in several smaller pieces, including the Wyoming portion (including the small piece that extends into Montana) of the population, Uintah and Rich-Morgan-Summit Management Areas in Utah, and North Park and NWCO subpopulations in Colorado.

Wyoming Portion

This large population covers approximately two-thirds of the State of Wyoming. It extends into Montana, Idaho, Utah and Colorado (Utah and Colorado portions are described separately). The population is separated from adjacent populations by distance and topography (Garton *et al*. 2011). Sage-grouse habitats are expansive and relatively intact outside of areas of energy development. Despite the long-term declines in populations, implementation of the Wyoming Governor's Executive Order for sage-grouse may help alleviate these declines. The primary threats to this portion of the population are energy development and transfer, including both renewable and non-renewable resources, long-term drought, and brush eradication programs. Declines of sage-grouse near oil and gas fields in this area have been well documented (Lyon 2000; Holloran 2005; Holloran and Anderson; Kaiser 2006). Residential development has also been identified as a threat. Recent conservation actions, including the Wyoming Governor's Executive Order designating protective stipulations for core areas (PACs) and the implementation of conservation easements within these areas have reduced the threat risk to this area. Designated state core areas (PACs) adequately capture redundancy and representation for the Wyoming portion of this population. Due to the large size of this population, the presence of large, contiguous habitats, and regulatory measures providing habitat protection, this population is considered low risk.

The majority of habitat that supports the Montana portion of the Wyoming Basin population is identified as a PAC, both because of the relatively high density of sage-grouse in the area and the likely role this area plays connecting Montana's sage-grouse to Wyoming's birds. In Montana, this area is among the driest of sage-grouse habitats and has a higher prevalence of cheat-grass relative to other parts of Montana. Land use includes livestock grazing and a long history of oil limited production. This portion of the Wyoming Basin Population is relatively small but is within 20 miles of another core area in Wyoming.

Rich-Morgan-Summit

The Rich-Morgan-Summit Sage-grouse Management Area is located in Northeastern Utah, and is a part of the Wyoming Basin population, a significant population center for grouse in Utah,

Idaho, Colorado, and Wyoming. This management area also includes part of what is mapped in Garton *et al.* 2011 as Summit-Morgan Counties in Management Zone III. The area boundary was determined by consulting with adjacent states, Utah Division of Wildlife Resources, the Morgan-Summit Adaptive Resources Management Local Sage-grouse Working Group, and the Rich County Coordinated Resource Management Sage-grouse Local Working Group and follows vegetation types usable by sage-grouse. This portion of the population is regarded as stable with potential for growth. Based on a ten-year average count of males on leks, the area had an estimated 1,223 males as of 2011. Sage-grouse in this area show resiliency to known threats. Key threats to sage-grouse include invasive species, loss of agricultural operations, predation, residential development, and habitat fragmentation through recreational development. In conjunction with populations in Wyoming, the management area is considered low risk.

Uintah

The Uintah Sage-grouse Management Area is located in northeastern Utah. This management area had an estimated 452 males on leks as of 2011. Within the northern portion of this area is the Diamond Mountain and Browns Park population, a significant population center for sage-grouse in Utah, Colorado, and Wyoming. The central and southern portions of the management area contain fragmented populations with minimal connectivity and low potential for habitat improvement. The Management Area boundary was determined by consulting with Utah Division of Wildlife Resources and the Uinta Basin Adaptive Resource Management Local Working Group, and follows vegetation types usable by sage-grouse. This portion of the Wyoming Basin population is regarded as stable with a potential for growth and also has strong connectivity with other portions of the population. Sage-grouse in the Management Area show resiliency to known threats. Key threats to sage-grouse include predation, wildfire, invasive species, noxious weeds, disease, loss of agricultural operations, and habitat fragmentation (naturally occurring, but not topographical, and from existing and future anthropogenic uses). In concert with the remaining portions of this population, the management area is considered low risk.

North Park

This portion of the Wyoming Basin population is located in North Park, Jackson County, Colorado. In North Park (NP), representation and redundancy appear to be captured well. Priority areas for conservation capture 91 percent of the occupied range in this population and include 100 percent of all known active leks and 100 percent of habitat that was modeled "high probability of use" within 4 miles of a lek that has been active within the last 10 years. Historically, no significant threats were apparent to this population. However, there is renewed interest in oil development in the area. In addition, a large portion (29 percent) of public land in PACs has been leased for energy development. North Park has overlapping energy and mineral resources and thus could experience natural gas, coal bed methane, and oil extraction. Although present, the other identified threats are less than other portions of the population. The habitat within PACs is in fairly good condition, and a large portion is on public lands. This is likely Colorado's most resilient area of occupied sage-grouse habitat. Long -term data trends (since the early 1970's) indicate this population has fluctuated roughly between 500 and 1,500 males. This subpopulation is considered low risk.

Northwest Colorado

In the northwest Colorado portion of this population, representation and redundancy appear to be captured adequately. Priority areas for conservation capture 56 percent of the occupied range and also include 95 percent of all known active leks and 95 percent of habitat that was modeled "high probability of use" within 4 miles of a lek that has been active within the last 10 years. Most of the sub-management zones within this portion of the population have some connectivity with other portions of this population. This is Colorado's largest area of sage-grouse occupancy and is considered to be at low risk of extirpation. The northern portion is likely to be more resilient than the southeastern portions of this population because of habitat condition and connectivity. There is more habitat fragmentation in the southeastern portion of this population. According to lek count data, the long-term trend appears to be stable, despite substantial fluctuations. Population peaks have occurred in 1960-70, 1978-80, and in the mid-2000s.

MANAGEMENT ZONE III: SOUTHERN GREAT BASIN

This management zone includes populations in California, Nevada, and Utah. The California populations in this Management Zone are described separately in the Bi-State DPS section (see below) and the Summit Morgan Counties population is described in Management Zone II. The populations in this management zone include Southern Great Basin, Northeast Interior, Sheeprock, Quinn Canyon Range, South Central Utah, Northeast Interior Utah, Emery, and Northwest Interior. Garton *et al.* (2011) predicted a 0.0 percent chance this Management Zone will fall below 200 males by 2037, and a 7.8 percent chance it would fall below 200 males by 2107. Landownership in this zone is predominately BLM (71 percent), followed by private (13 percent) and others (Knick 2011). This zone is part of a stronghold for sage-grouse (that includes Management Zones III, IV, and V) because the three zones contain the largest area of habitat range-wide with low similarity to extirpated portions of the range (Wisdom *et al.* 2011). Despite the fact this zone has large areas of sagebrush habitat in Nevada this area faces large risks due to wildfire. Since it is difficult to restore burned habitat (Pyke 2011), the management approach for this area should provide a cushion to deal with fire events that are expected to occur but are not predictable in their location, extent, and outcome.

Northeast Interior Utah

This population is located entirely in Utah and has been divided into the Strawberry Valley and Carbon Management Areas.

Strawberry Valley

The Strawberry Valley Sage-grouse Management Area is located in central Utah, and is a significant population center for sage-grouse in Utah. This management area had an estimated 82 males on leks as of 2011. The area boundary was determined by consulting with DWR and the Strawberry Valley Adaptive Resource Management Local Working Group, and follows vegetation types usable by sage-grouse. Significant restoration efforts have been conducted on this population and it is the most intensively managed in Utah. This population is regarded as stable with a high potential for growth. Sage-grouse in this area had suffered significant reductions in populations, but concentrated restoration efforts have resulted in significant population growth. Due to its smaller size, Strawberry Valley is considered at-risk.

Carbon

The Carbon Sage-grouse Management Area is located in the northern portion of the Colorado Plateau in central Utah. This management area had an estimated 119 males on leks as of 2011. The area is characterized by highly broken terrain, with deep canyons and mid-elevation plateaus. Telemetry studies in the area suggest that occasionally sage-grouse migrate to and from the adjoining Strawberry Valley portion of this population. The area boundary was determined by buffering active leks with topographic imagery, and adding areas of known winter use. Key threats include habitat loss and fragmentation due to a variety of factors including energy development, wildfire, invasive species, and predation. West Nile Virus has been reported in Carbon in the last 10 years. The management area is at-risk.

Emery

The Emery population in Utah is considered the Emery Sage-grouse Management Area and is also known as the Sanpete-Emery Counties population in Garton *et al.* (2011). This population had an estimated 30 males on leks as of 2011. Small, mostly isolated sage-grouse populations occupy high elevation sagebrush steppe on the eastern slope of the Wastach Plateau. Although no direct movement between these areas has been documented, this population is relatively close to the South Central Utah population (Parker Mountain portion). This population includes all currently used habitat and corridors connecting this habitat. Key threats to the population include woody species encroachment, wildfire, invasive species, predation, and habitat fragmentation. Due to its smaller size, Emery is considered at-risk.

Sheeprock

The Sheeprock population in Utah is a relatively isolated population center also known as the Sheeprock Mountains Management Area. Garton *et al.* (2011) refers to this as the Toole-Juab Counties population. This population had an estimated 102 males on leks as of 2011. The area boundary was determined by consulting with the West Desert Adaptive Resource Management local working group and Utah Division of Wildlife Resources, and follows vegetation types usable by sage-grouse. This population is regarded as stable with a potential for growth. Sage-grouse in this area show resiliency to known threats. Key threats to sage-grouse include wildfire, invasive species (cheatgrass and knapweeds), potential loss of riparian areas due to water piping, predation, and habitat fragmentation (dispersed recreation and pinyon-juniper encroachment). The management area is considered high risk.

South Central Utah

The population is located entirely within Utah and is one of the State's largest. It has been divided into three portions for management purposes including the Greater Parker Mountain, Panguitch, and Bald Hills.

Greater Parker Mountain

The Greater Parker Mountain Sage-grouse Management Area portion of the South Central Utah population is located on the Awapa Plateau and nearby environments. The Greater Parker Mountain Local Area Working Group was established in 1996 and is the longest operational working group in Utah. The boundaries of this portion of the population were refined based on 15 years of greater sage-grouse radio telemetry studies which included research on species' vital rates, survival, and seasonal movements. Boundary refinements included coordination with the working groups and the Utah Division of Wildlife Resources. This area had an estimated 821 males on leks in 2011. Because of these long-term research studies in this area, more is known about sage-grouse population dynamics, seasonal habitat use, population threats, and abatement strategies in this area than in other areas of Utah. This portion of the population includes all connected currently used habitats and corridors connecting these habitats. Key sage-grouse threats identified include: 1) loss or degradation of habitat (primarily due to vegetation succession), 2) conversion of habitat (sagebrush to pinyon-juniper or cheatgrass at the lower elevations), 3) increased risk of predation because of expansion of, or changes in, the native predator community in response to anthropogenic factors, and 4) habitat fragmentation from loss or degradation of habitat that results in a loss of sage-grouse habitat connectivity.

Panguitch

The Panguitch portion of the South Central Utah population is referred to as the Panguitch Management Area. It incorporates more than a dozen leks, often inter-connected. This area had an estimated 304 males on leks in 2011. This portion of the population is distributed north-south in a series of linked valleys and benches, and constrained by mountains and canyons. There is a large range in the number of males in attendance among these leks. Movement of sage-grouse from one valley or bench to another among seasons is necessary to meet their seasonal habitat requirements in the highly variable annual weather conditions of this region. This area has the highest potential for increase in Utah due to habitat treatments to remove pinyon-juniper. Key threats to sage-grouse in this area are increased predator populations, vegetation management (conflicting uses or lack of), energy development, and residential/commercial development.

Bald Hills

The Bald Hills portion of the South Central Utah population is referred to as the Bald Hills Management Area. This area had an estimated 68 males on leks in 2011. Currently, sage-grouse in the area are constrained by vegetation fragmentation and human development. However, future improvements could connect this population to the Southern Great Basin population (Hamlin Valley portion) to the west. This portion of the South Central Utah population is regarded as stable with a high potential for growth. Sage-grouse in this area show resiliency to known threats. Key threats include wildfire, increased predator populations, vegetation management (conflicting uses or lack of), and energy development.

Northwest Interior

This population is largely within Pershing County, Nevada, but also incorporates a portion of western Lander County and southeastern Humboldt County. Few PACs are mapped within this population other than some habitats within the Sonoma Range in southeastern Humboldt County, the Tobin Range in eastern Pershing County, and the Fish Creek Range in western Lander County. Priority areas for conservation identified within these ranges largely cover all remaining suitable habitat for sage-grouse. There were not enough data for Garton *et al.* (2011) to conduct an analysis on population trends or persistence estimates. The largest sub-populations within this area are within the Sonoma-Tobin complex and the Fish Creek Range. Lek count information from both of these areas suggest that there is less than 500 birds in each one of these populations and the potential for connectivity appears low, but possible. Other sub-populations within this area (e.g., Eugene Mountains, East Range, Humboldt Range, Majuba Mountain, and Trinity Ranges) have extremely low populations (<50 birds) with some of these ranges having populations that are extirpated due to severe wildfire and inability of the habitat to recover. Much of these areas are now monotypic stands of cheatgrass and tansy mustard. Overall, this population is high risk.

Southern Great Basin

This population contains the largest number of sage-grouse within Management Zone 3. It is relatively expansive and divided into a Nevada portion and Ibapah and Hamlin Valley portions within Utah.

Nevada

The Nevada portion of this population contains the largest number of sage-grouse in this population delineation. Suitable habitats are somewhat uncharacteristic of sage-grouse habitats because use areas are disjunct, but connected. This is due to the "basin and range" topography that is characteristic of this region. Lower elevation valley bottoms often are dominated by playas and salt desert shrub vegetation, but transcend quickly into sagebrush dominated benches, which often comprises the breeding and winter habitat. Moving up in elevation, pinyon-juniper woodlands dominate the mid-elevation and gives way to little sagebrush, mountain big sagebrush and mountain shrub communities used by sage-grouse as nesting and brood rearing habitat in the higher elevations (> 2,200 m).

Priority areas for conservation (PACs) adequately capture important use areas for this population as all use areas were mapped to the greatest extent practical under the time constraints given to complete a map for the BLM's interim guidance. Redundancy and representation exist within this population, largely because it covers a large geographic area. Most populations appear to be connected as indicated through recent telemetry investigations and the availability of suitable habitat between sub-populations within this region. Resiliency of the habitat is in question due to threats, either projected or realized, in the lower elevation habitats, as explained below.

Garton *et al.* (2011) determined that this population has declined by 19 percent from the period 1965-69 through 2000-2007 and that average rates of population change were <1.0 for three of the eight analysis periods from 1965-2007. In addition, Garton *et al.* (2011) determined that this population has a two percent chance of declining below 200 males within the next 30 years and a 78 percent chance of declining below 200 males within 100 years (by 2107).

Some of the historic habitat available to sage-grouse within this population has transitioned to pinyon-juniper woodlands. Miller and Tausch (2001) estimated that the area of pinyon-juniper woodlands has increased approximately 10-fold throughout the western United States since the late 1800s. Additionally, Wisdom *et al.* (2005) determined that 35 percent of the sagebrush area in the eastern Great Basin is at high risk to future displacement by pinyon-juniper woodlands and that mountain big sagebrush appeared to be most at risk, which could have meaningful impacts to sage-grouse brood rearing habitats within the upper elevations of mountain ranges within this region. In addition to this threat, much of the Great Basin is also susceptible to sagebrush displacement by cheatgrass. The most at risk vegetative community in this region is Wyoming-basin big sagebrush (Wisdom *et al.* 2005) located predominately within the lower elevation benches of mountain ranges. In some areas, this condition has already been realized and the future risk for existing sagebrush habitats is moderate to high. This threatens both breeding and winter habitats for sage-grouse. For example, in a study conducted within this region (in Eureka County, NV), Blomberg *et al.* (2012) determined that sage-grouse leks that were not impacted by exotic grasslands experienced recruitment levels that were six times greater than those impacted by exotic grasslands. Additionally, this study found that drought is a major contributor to reduced recruitment and low population growth within the Southern Great Basin. Other threats such as mining and infrastructure have the potential to affect this sage-grouse population due to mine expansions, as well as new mines and the infrastructure associated with them. Existing mining claims are virtually ubiquitous throughout the Southern Great Basin PAC. Overall, sage-grouse in the Southern Great Basin in Nevada are potentially at-risk.

Ibapah

The Ibapah portion of the Southern Great Basin population is also referred to as the Ibapah Management Area and is located in northwestern Utah. This area had an estimated 39 males on leks as of 2011, primarily on Goshute Tribal lands. The area boundary was determined by consulting with Nevada, the West Desert Adaptive Resource Management Local Area Working Group, and the Utah Division of Wildlife Resources and follows vegetation types used by sage-grouse. Sage-grouse in this area show resiliency to known threats. Key threats to sage-grouse are fire, invasive species (cheatgrass and knapweeds), potential loss of riparian areas due to water piping, predation, and habitat fragmentation (from dispersed recreation and pinyon-juniper encroachment).

Hamlin Valley

The Hamlin Valley portion of the Southern Great Basin population is also referred to as the Hamlin Valley Management Area. It is located in southwestern Utah, on the border of Utah and Nevada and is important due to its connectivity with other portions of the population. Although currently isolated from other habitat areas in Utah, habitat restoration could link this population to the South Central Utah population. This area consists of a relatively small number of birds (i.e., 89 males in 2011) that use less than 10 leks throughout the habitat area. This portion of the population is regarded as moderately stable with a high potential for growth. Key threats include wildfire, increased predator populations, vegetation management, wild horse management, and habitat fragmentation.

Quinn Canyon Range

This is a very small and isolated population located in southeastern Nevada. There were not enough data for Garton *et al.* (2011) to conduct an analysis on population trends or persistence. Two to three leks have been identified in this area, but there is very little information associated with these sites and most of this information is anecdotal. Habitat within this area has been compromised by pinyon-juniper encroachment. No PACs were identified for this population largely because the majority of vegetative associations are either salt desert shrub communities or pinyon-juniper stands. Very little sagebrush exists within this population. Overall this is a high risk population.

MANAGEMENT ZONE IV: SNAKE RIVER PLAIN

This zone represents one of the largest areas of connected sage-grouse habitat, as demonstrated by Knick *et al.* (2011), and supports the largest population of sage-grouse outside of the Wyoming Basin (Garton *et al.* 2011). The Snake River Plain management zone includes sage-grouse populations in Oregon, Idaho, Nevada, Utah and Montana. Garton *et al.* (2011) predicted a 10.5 percent chance this Management Zone will fall below 200 males by 2037, and a 39.7 percent chance it would fall below 200 males by 2107.

Baker

The Baker population has approximately the same distribution as the area covered by the Baker administrative unit identified in Oregon's Sage-grouse Conservation Strategy (Hagen 2011b). The Baker spring population was estimated to be 872 -1,650 birds in 2010, the smallest extant population of sage-grouse that is exclusively in Oregon. Garton *et al.* (2011) based their Baker population assessment on minimum estimate of 137 birds in 2007 and estimated a 61.9% chance there will be fewer than 50 birds in the population by the year 2037, similarly, there is 66.8% chance of fewer than 50 birds by 2137. The Oregon Department of Fish and Wildlife lek counts indicated more than 300 males in Baker County in 2011. Since systematic counts began in 1989, the number of counted males/lek has remained relatively stable (Hagen 2011b). Due to habitat and topography it has been assumed the Baker population has little connectivity with other sage-grouse populations. Recent telemetry information suggests that at least some birds move between the Weiser population in Idaho and the Baker population.

The Baker population is more at risk and likely less resilient, since connectivity to other populations appears limited (future genetics work will help clarify this). There is no redundancy in this population as all birds are believed to be in one general area. For the entire population, the environmental similarity to extirpated populations is high (Wisdom *et al.* 2011). Most (68%) of the sage-grouse habitat for the Baker population is in private ownership and 31% is administered by BLM (Hagen 2011b). This is the largest proportion of privately managed sage-grouse habitat for any population in Oregon. Consequently, there are limited regulatory mechanisms in place, making it uncertain as to whether state-recommended conservation measures and practices will be applied on the majority of lands within this population.

More than 80% of the historical sagebrush habitat for the Baker Population remains available today but steeper habitat and rugged topography reduces the suitability for sage-grouse. Nearly 300,000 acres in this region were identified as priority areas for conservation, and includes much of the current range of the Baker population. Invasive weeds and juniper encroachment are considered to be the primary threats to this population (Hagen 2011b), but other threats to this population include renewable energy development (primarily wind), energy transmission, and OHV recreation. Recently, thousands of acres of juniper have been treated in this region to benefit sage-grouse and other sagebrush obligates. Most of the area used by this population has been mapped as priority habitat.

East-Central Idaho

Areas within the East Idaho Uplands in the Blackfoot River drainage downstream from Blackfoot Reservoir have historically provided popular sites for greater sage-grouse hunters. The area is generally characterized by a high proportion of private and state land and a local working group has been actively pursuing conservation measures. Nevertheless little information is available on sage-grouse populations other than some limited location and attendance data on a few leks. No lek routes have been established within this area that would allow consistent monitoring of sage-grouse populations. This lack of data is largely due to very difficult access in most years during winter and spring. Analysis of limited data by Garton *et al.* (2011) suggests that this population has a low probability of persistence. Although causal observation and some historic data suggest the study area provides adequate breeding and nesting habitat, sage-grouse numbers appear to be very low. Initial summer surveys in 2011 suggested sage-grouse were reasonably widespread throughout the area. However, given the apparent overall quality of the habitat, sage-grouse numbers seem surprisingly low and difficult to explain. Factors that could act to reduce sage-grouse populations in this area include sagebrush treatments in breeding habitat, West Nile virus, and loss or fragmentation of winter range. Overall this population is considered high risk.

Southwest Montana

The Southwest Montana Population occurs in Beaverhead and Madison Counties, within a 60 mile radius of Dillon, MT. Segments of this population also make seasonal migrations into Idaho. Garton *et al.* (2011) analyzed the Southwest Montana population as 4 separate smaller populations (i.e., Bannack, Wisdom, Red Rock, and Bridges), but did not provide an analysis of the overall population. Telemetry data, however, has demonstrated considerable intermingling between each of these lek complexes, clarifying that these birds represent a single population (and could be more accurately described as four sub-populations). Priority areas for conservation encompass about 80 percent of the habitat associated with the Southwest Montana Population. These PACs were identified because of the relatively high density of sage-grouse and the genetic conduit this area provides with Idaho's birds. Habitat threats are generally limited to improper grazing management, isolated sagebrush control efforts, and expansion of conifers into sage-grouse habitat in localized instances. Habitat conversion on the Idaho side of this Management Zone may also affect this population to some extent. Both the Centennial and Big Hole valleys are focus areas for native habitat conservation for grayling, sage-grouse and other wildlife, resulting in considerable acreage enrolled in long-term and perpetual conservation agreements with private landowners. Given this population's size, limited habitat threats, and ties to Idaho's birds, the Southwest Montana population is characterized as being at a low level of risk.

Snake-Salmon-Beaverhead

Recent data indicates this large population extends into southwestern Montana. This area contains a large amount of publicly managed land (largely BLM and USFS). Within the southern portion of this population, wildfires and invasive species have continued to reduce the quality of habitat. The mountain Valley portions of this population appear to have relatively stable habitats. Thus far, energy development is very limited and there are few wild horses. A recent rate of change analysis indicates this population has been stable to increasing from 2007 to 2010. Garton *et al.* (2011) indicated that this population had virtually no chance of declining below 500 in the next 100 years. Population analysis indicates that sage-grouse have fluctuated around 5,000 males since 1992. Because of relatively large numbers of birds and stable to increasing populations, this population is considered low risk.

Belt Mountains

This population occurs within a broad intermountain valley that extends roughly from White Sulfur Springs south toward Livingston, within Meagher and Park Counties. This population experienced considerable habitat conversion to small grain cropping in the late 1960s through the 1980s, involving at least one key sage-grouse wintering area (Swenson *et al.* 1987). Ironically, some of these croplands have since been enrolled into the Conservation Reserve Program (CRP) but natural sagebrush recovery appears minimal. Garton *et al.* (2011) were unable to develop any population predictions due to a lack of sufficient data. This population is at least 50 miles distant from the nearest adjacent population. Timbered and mountainous terrain and expansive non-habitat barriers further isolate this population in nearly every direction. Sagebrush control projects, primarily using herbicides, and conversion to cropland and domestic seeded pastures have continued to affect portions of the remaining habitat during the past 20 years. More recently, isolated housing developments and limited drilling for oil and/or gas resources have impacted a relatively small portion of remaining sagebrush grassland habitats in this area. The small population size, isolation from other populations, and a history of significant habitat perturbations, some of which continue but perhaps at a slower rate, places this population as high risk.

Weiser

This small population in western Idaho did not have sufficient data to allow analysis by Garton *et al.* (2011). However, 2010 data indicated the area had 14 occupied leks. Recently some connection with the Baker, Oregon population has been documented. The area is generally characterized by a high proportion of private land and a local working group has been actively pursuing conservation measures. Because of relatively few birds, fragmented habitat and a large portion of existing habitat on private lands, this population is considered at risk.

Northern Great Basin

The Northern Great Basin population is a large population in Oregon, Idaho, Nevada, and Utah. It has been divided into the large portion in Oregon, Idaho, and Nevada and a smaller portion in northwestern Utah called the Box Elder area. This area contains a large amount of publicly managed land (largely BLM). The area also includes among the least fragmented and largest sagebrush dominated landscapes within the extant range of sage-grouse (Knick and Hanser 2011). However, the northern and eastern portions of the population are more environmentally similar to areas where sage-grouse have been extirpated (Wisdom *et al.* 2011).

Despite efforts to manage wildfire risks, wildfires and invasive species have continued to reduce the quality of habitat in portions of this area. Idaho's Murphy Fire Complex recently affected roughly 600,000 acres of habitat for this population. The 2012 Long Draw fire in Oregon affected 582,000 acres; 455,000 acres were considered either Core or Low Density sage-grouse habitat under Oregon's conservation strategy, of which 213,000 acres in a PAC.

A recent rate of change analysis indicated that at least part of this large population has been stable to increasing from 2007-2010. Garton *et al.* (2011) indicated that this population had virtually no chance of declining below 50 in 30 or 100 years. Population analysis indicated that sage-grouse will fluctuate around a carrying capacity that will decline from an estimated 6,770 males in 2007 to 1787 males in 2037 if current trends continue (Garton *et al.* 2011).

Redundancy and representation appear to be captured adequately in the PACs. In Oregon, PACs capture 95 percent of all known breeding locations, 98 percent of known wintering locations (which was expected since this was based on telemetry data), and 89 percent of known summer locations. Priority areas for conservation and low density (non-priority but managed) habitat combined capture all but three percent of known summer, one percent of known breeding, and one percent of known wintering habitat. Oregon PACs also considered the need to maintain a network of connected habitats.

The Nevada portion of the Northern Great Basin population represents the largest, most contiguous concentration of sage-grouse in Nevada and includes the Santa Rosa, Desert, Tuscarora, North Fork, O'Neil Basin, Islands, Snake and Gollaher Population Management Units. Portions of this area are well connected with Oregon, Idaho and Utah. Fire and invasive annual grasses are the major threats to the Nevada portion of this population. Since 2000, over 800,000 acres of sagebrush habitats have burned in this region. Rehabilitation efforts and the higher elevation/higher precipitation zones for some recent wildfires have led to expedited habitat recovery that is once again being utilized by sage-grouse demonstrating at least some resiliency for this portion of the population.. Winter habitat in some areas has been compromised although recent winter snowpack has been below average, allowing birds to utilize an expanded area. The Gollaher and Tuscarora population management units have been prone to wildfire and are more susceptible to invasive species such as cheatgrass. Mining and infrastructure have potential to pose additional threats to sage-grouse habitat as gold prices have increased 112% over the last 5 years and mining claims are numerous within the Nevada portion of the Northern Great Basin.

Oregon represents the western part of this large population which is shared with southern Idaho, NE Nevada, and NW Utah. Within Oregon, this represents one of the largest populations. The delineation of the Northern Great Basin population doesn't correspond well to any existing assessment for Oregon, but does include almost all of the Vale administrative unit, as well as portions of the Burns administrative unit. In Oregon alone, the spring population in the Northern Great Basin is likely several thousand birds, with 2011 spring lek counts approaching 3,000 males (in the Beulah, Malheur River, Owyhee, and eastern portion of Whitehorse Wildlife Management Units). Garton *et al.* (2011) estimated for the Northern Great Basin a minimum population estimate of 9,114 males in 2007 (includes S. ID, NE NV, NW UT). Modeling suggested there is a 2.5% chance birds will drop below 500 by the year 2037, but a 99.7% chance the population will be below 500 by 2137 (Garton *et al.* 2011). Loss of sagebrush habitat has been and continues to be threat to the population in Oregon. Between 1963 and 1974, 500,000 acres of sagebrush habitat was seeded to crested wheatgrass or sprayed with herbicide, and 1,600 water developments and 463 miles of pipeline were installed in the Vale District BLM's area for the Vale project. More recently, wildfire is the most significant threat to landscape scale losses of sagebrush habitat as indicated by the previously mentioned 582,000 acre Long Draw fire of 2012. In conjunction with fire, invasive weeds are also one of the greatest risks the 4+ million acres of sagebrush habitat for this population in Oregon. More than

580,000 acres is already dominated by invasive species (Hagen 2011b). In many instances, these areas were historically dominated by Wyoming big sagebrush habitat. Other threats in this region include mining development, renewable energy development, transmission, and juniper encroachment at higher elevations. West Nile virus has also been consistently detected in mosquitoes in this region (http://public.health.oregon.gov/) and the population was subjected to the largest known West Nile virus mortality event involving sage-grouse in Oregon (2006). Despite efforts to manage wildfire risks, wildfires and invasive species have continued to reduce the quality of habitat in portions of this area. Largely due to the landscape altering potential of very large wildfires, with recent years as evidence, overall this part of the population is potentially at risk.

Box Elder

The Box Elder portion of the Northern Great Basin population is located in northwestern Utah. This area is referred to as the Box Elder Management Area. It had an estimated 755 males on leks as of 2011. This population is regarded as stable with a potential for growth. Key threats include wildfire, invasive species, loss of agricultural operations, and habitat fragmentation. The area can likely sustain increases in sage-grouse populations with continued reclamation and restoration. As a result, this area should be a high priority for funding of habitat enhancement. Because this area is a portion of the large Northern Great Basin population, it is potentially at risk.

Sawtooth

This small population in central Idaho did not have sufficient data to allow analysis by Garton *et al.* (2011). No occupied leks are known to exist at this time. This area is largely encompassed by the Sawtooth National Recreation Area and includes a high proportion of public land. This population declined to one male on one lek in 1986 and was subsequently increased by translocation during the mid-1980s. Overall this population is at high risk.

MANAGEMENT ZONE V: NORTHERN GREAT BASIN

There are four sage-grouse populations identified in this management zone, including Central Oregon, Klamath, Warm Springs Valley, and the Western Great Basin. Garton *et al.* (2011) predicted a 2.1 percent chance this Management Zone will fall below 200 males by 2037, and a 29.0 percent chance it would fall below 200 males by 2107. Only two of the populations (Central Oregon and Western Great Basin) had sufficient information for a population assessment by Garton *et al.* (2011). BLM lands are a major constituent of sagebrush landscapes in the Northern Great Basin (62 percent), followed by private (21 percent), Forest Service (10 percent), state (8 percent), and then other ownerships (Knick 2011). This zone is part of a stronghold for sage-grouse (that includes Management Zones III, IV, and V) because the three zones contain the largest area of habitat range-wide with low similarity to extirpated portions of the range (Wisdom *et al.* 2011).

Central Oregon

The Central Oregon population has approximately the same distribution as the area covered by the Prineville administrative unit identified in Oregon's Sage-grouse Conservation Strategy. Approximately 700,000 acres of habitat for the Central Oregon population has been identified as priority areas for conservation. This is a relatively large population, with the minimum spring population estimated at 1,775-2,084 birds in 2010 (Hagen 2011b). The population has declined steadily since 1980 (average, -0.004 percent/yr [Hagen 2011b]). There is a 15.2 percent chance the population will decline below 500 by 2037, and a 91.3 percent chance that fewer than 500 birds will be in the population by 2137 (Garton et al. 2011).

This population is estimated to have only 53 percent of historic sagebrush habitat, having lost more historic habitat than any other sage-grouse administrative unit in Oregon. The area also has more privately owned sage-grouse habitat (48 percent) than most other sage-grouse management zone populations in Oregon. This population faces a wide suite of threats, including juniper encroachment, (Freese 2009) which threatens over 900,000 acres of the 1.8 million acres of sagebrush habitat in in this area (Hagen 2011b). Additional threats include invasive weeds, renewable energy development (both wind and geothermal), transmission, roads, OHV recreation, and residential development. Projections based on historic trends suggest this population is at risk, but in the last 2 years there have been a number of positive developments including thousands of acres of habitat improvement under the NRCS's Sage-grouse Initiative and increasing local interest sage-grouse conservation. Juniper encroachment does threaten connectivity with other Oregon populations to the south and east (Hagen 2011b).
Based on Garton et al. (2011), this population appears fairly resilient in 30 years, but not in 100 years. Redundancy and representation appear to be captured adequately. PACs capture 95 percent of all known sage-grouse breeding locations, 98 percent of known wintering locations, and 89 percent of known summer locations. Priority areas for conservation and low density (non-priority but managed) habitat combined capture all but three percent of known summer, one percent of known breeding, and one percent of known wintering habitat. Since this population's habitat/landscape appears more similar to landscapes in extirpated populations than extant populations, particularly in the northwest extant of range (Wisdom et al. 2011), we suggest retaining all priority habitats for this populations. Most of the sites within this population (with the possible exception of the southwestern site) probably have some connectivity with other sites in this population, though verification from genetics is lacking. Although much of the known habitat is mapped, we suggest retaining all PACs in Central Oregon.

Klamath

The Klamath population is all that remains of a population that once extended from northern California through southern Oregon. The California portion includes the Devil's Garden Area of Modoc County, which had at least 46 known leks as recently as the 1970s, and was well connected to populations in Oregon and the Western Great Basin. By the early 2000s, only one known lek remained on the Clear Lake National Wildlife Refuge in California, with less than 10 males. Since 2005, birds have been translocated from Oregon and Nevada to the refuge to prevent extirpation. A small amount of priority habitat is mapped for the area where birds currently exist, but not connected to the Western Great Basin or Central Oregon populations. Redundancy is not adequate and resistance is poor. This population is at immediate risk of extinction without continued augmentation. There is no priority habitat mapped in this population for Oregon because we have not documented birds there recently.

There are no priority areas for conservation mapped for this population in Oregon because sage-grouse in the Oregon part of the Klamath population are thought to be extirpated. As recently as the early 1990's, a few birds attended leks in Oregon, but there have been no confirmed sightings since 1993, despite periodic survey efforts. The Klamath population was likely an extension of the population in northeast California and likely had limited connectivity with sage-grouse populations in eastern Oregon due to barriers of unsuitable habitat. Habitat in both California and Oregon is severely compromised by juniper encroachment, wildfire, and invasive grasses. Significant juniper treatments have taken place in and around the area currently occupied by sage-grouse and in the former Oregon range. There is potential for limited range expansion for sage-grouse in the future.

Warm Springs Valley

This is a small population that exists in southern Washoe County within the Virginia Population Management Unit. Only two confirmed active leks comprise this population; however, lek size is relatively large (average of over 40). The identified PACs encompass the majority of use areas. Extensive research has been conducted within this particular Population Management Unit. Some individuals have dispersed to the southern portion of the western Great Basin population during the winter, so there is the possibility of genetic interchange. There is an indication of this from work conducted by Oyler-McCance *et al.* (2005) suggesting a relationship with the Lassen population in California. Representation and redundancy are limited within this population due to its small size, proximity to urbanized setting and threats from invasive species.

The Warm Springs population in southern Washoe County may be close to a threshold if additional threats occur. This population is very close to urban areas, has experienced large wildfire and energy development in the form of a utility scale transmission line (345kV Alturas line) and water transfer pipeline (Vidler Water), and is experiencing some pinyon-juniper encroachment. However, the primary area used by sage-grouse in the population (Spanish Flat) remains intact and benefits from higher elevation precipitation regimes. Overall, this is population is at risk.

Western Great Basin

The Western Great Basin population is shared among southeastern Oregon, northeastern California and northwestern Nevada. Range-wide for sage-grouse, this area contains one of four remaining large intact expanses of sagebrush habitat and connects south-central Oregon with northwest Nevada, with most of the sagebrush dominated landscape in Oregon (Knick and Hanser 2011). Habitat fragmentation increases to the south and west in the population, with northeast California having a high similarity with portions of extirpated range (Wisdom *et al.* 2011). Garton *et al.* (2011) estimated for the Western Great Basin a minimum population estimate of 5,904 males in 2007 (includes NE CA, NW NV). Over 8 analysis periods conducted by Garton *et al.* (2011), average rates of change were <1.0 in 3 of those periods and the minimum population estimate was determined to be 5,904 males in 2007 based on counts at 393 leks. Modeling suggested there is a 6.4 percent chance birds will drop below 500 by the year 2037, but a 99.1 percent chance the population will be below 500 by 2137 (Garton *et al.* 2011). The Western Great Basin is the most resilient population in Management Zone 5, but reducing threats alone is not likely to ensure long-term persistence in some areas. Resiliency needs to be improved in the California and Nevada portions of the Western Great Basin with increased habitat suitability in terms of shrub densities and native grasses and forbs.

Oregon's portion of the population has some of the best habitat and highest sage-grouse densities in the state, including Hart Mountain National Antelope Refuge and Trout Creek Mountains, though habitat in the Trout Creeks was likely compromised by 2012 fires. The delineation of the Western Great Basin population doesn't correspond well to any existing assessment for Oregon, but does include almost all of the Lakeview administrative unit, as well as portions of the Burns and Vale administrative units. In just Oregon, the spring population in the Western Great Basin likely exceeded 10,000 birds in 2010 (interpolation from Hagen 2011b). In the Oregon, >80 percent of the historical sage-grouse habitat remains intact, and most of the habitat is in public ownership (Hagen 2011b). In the Lakeview administration unit, which comprises most of the Western Great Basin population in Oregon, about 78 percent of the region is administered by the BLM and the FWS manages more than 278,000 acres. Invasive weeds, fire, and juniper encroachment (particularly on the western edge) represent the greatest risks to this population. Renewable energy development (wind and geothermal) and wild horses have been identified as a threat to sage-grouse habitat in portions of Oregon's (e.g., Steens, Dry Valley/Jack Mountain Action Areas) Western Great Basin population. Given the majority of this population occupies federal land, proper and proactive habitat management could ensure the persistence of this sage-grouse population well into the future. Redundancy and representation appear to be captured adequately in the Oregon portion of this population given that priority habitats include most of the known distribution of birds (see rationale in Central above).

The California portion of the Western Great Basin includes the majority of the Buffalo-Skedaddle Population Management Unit. Priority habitat in California includes 100 percent of known sage-grouse distribution. This population was part of a much larger population that was connected to the Klamath population into the 1970's. Habitat degradation, including juniper expansion and spread of exotic grasses has been extraordinary in this region, resulting in range contraction over the past few decades. In August, 2012, the Rush Fire burned more than 265,000 acres of PACs in California and more than 313,000 acres including Nevada. Most of the largest leks and important nesting habitats were within the fire perimeter. Furthermore, the fire was focused on the East Lassen area to the east of Highway 395, which connects to the Western Great Basin Population in Nevada. The remaining area occupied by grouse in Central Lassen on the western periphery of the range may be further isolated by this fire. The extant population was considered well connected prior to the fire, but connectivity post-fire is unclear. The California portion of the Western Great Basin had experienced recent positive population trends, demonstrating that the population could exhibit positive growth rates during years of favorable environmental conditions. However, habitat suitability pre-fire was considered low (Davis 2012) and was in need of improvement to increase resistance of this population. The full effects of this large-scale wildfire are unclear at this time. The Nevada portion of this population includes the Buffalo/Skedaddle, Massacre, Vya, Sheldon, Black Rock, Pine Forest and Lone Willow Population Management Units. Currently identified priority habitat encompasses an area greater than the 85 percent core breeding density as reconstructed by the Nevada Department of Wildlife using methods described by Doherty *et al.* (2010), but utilizing the 10-year average for lek attendance rather than the most recent peak. Redundancy and representation are adequately captured both within the Nevada portion of this population and certainly within the Western Great Basin population as identified by Garton *et al.* (2011).

The Lone Willow portion of the Western Great Basin population (connected with Oregon) was affected by a very large wildfire in 2012. The Holloway Fire burned approximately 214,000 acres in Nevada and 245,000 acres in Oregon of which about 140,000 acres in Nevada and 221,000 acres in Oregon were considered important or essential sage-grouse habitat. The Miller Homestead fire in Oregon included an additional 162,000 acres of sagebrush habitat within its perimeter, 149,000 acres of which was identified as a PAC for the Western Great Basin population. Fire and annual grasses should be characterized as substantial and imminent threats within this portion of the population. Additionally, this area faces threats from lithium and uranium exploration and extraction. Along with infrastructure that may come with this potential development, it may be appropriate to characterize mining and infrastructure as substantial, non-imminent threats to this portion of the population.

Both the Massacre and Buffalo/Skedaddle Population Management Units face high risk due to invasive species being pervasive within the understory of lower elevation sagebrush communities. Improper livestock grazing practices and wild horse utilization have caused severe habitat degradation in some instances, especially with respect to meadow, spring and riparian habitats. Within the Massacre PMU, important information relative to habitat condition is contained within the BLM's Environmental Assessment for a Wild Horse Population Management Plan within the High Rock Complex (DOI-BLM-CA-N070-2011-04-EA). Appendix F of this document provided the results of Rangeland Health Assessments (RHAs) across five Herd Management Areas (HMAs). Within the "Standards for Biodiversity" sections of these RHAs, of the 28 sites assessed, 50% of them were not meeting biodiversity standards. This was mainly due to a lack of an adequate quantity of key deep-rooted perennial grasses such as Thurber's needlegrass, bluebunch wheatgrass and Idaho fescue, but also due to poor riparian condition as well. Whether or not this condition is the result of historic or current livestock grazing practices and/or wild horse utilization is debatable, but the fact that it continues to exist requires more appropriate management actions to improve the condition of the habitat. Since much of this region is susceptible to annual grass establishment, it is important that the perennial grass understory is maintained and perpetuated to help curtail the invasion of species like cheatgrass. This is supported by the findings of Blank and Morgan (2012) where, relative to controls, established perennial grasses significantly hindered the growth of cheatgrass. In addition to less than adequate upland conditions, this EA also found that riparian areas, spring and meadow complexes were damaged as well. The EA reports: "Riparian functional assessments completed in 2010 have determined that most riparian sites within the High Rock Complex are "Functional at Risk" (66%), and several other sites (17%) are rated as "Nonfunctional". This means that the majority of sites (83%) are in an obvious degraded condition. Sites rated as FAR are in danger of becoming "Nonfunctional" if the stresses and disturbances causing these conditions are allowed to continue. The dominant causal factors for riparian and wetland sites not being rated as PFC is grazing and trampling from livestock and wild horses. Many sites have recorded causal factors for not achieving PFC as continuous, year round use by wild horses.

Within the Sheldon National Wildlife Refuge, wild horses were rated as the highest risk to sage-grouse habitat quality by the Washoe-Lassen-Modoc local working group. This assessment was further justified within the Sheldon National Wildlife Refuge Comprehensive Conservation Plan (CCP) which identified management of feral horses and burros as the most important issue affecting the ability of the Service to fulfill the purposes for Sheldon Refuge (USFWS 2012). Additionally, an Environmental Assessment prepared by the USFWS (USFWS 2008) determined that wild horses and burros had direct adverse impacts to biological integrity, diversity and environmental health within Sheldon Refuge.

The Western Great Basin is most resilient in MZ5, but reducing threats alone is not likely to ensure long-term persistence in some areas. Resiliency needs to be improved in the California portion of the Western Great Basin with increased habitat suitability in terms of shrub densities and native grasses and forbs. Additionally, for this population to retain its resiliency, significant efforts are needed to ensure post-fire habitat recovery and prevent dominance of non-native vegetation. Overall this population is considered potentially at risk.

MANAGEMENT ZONE VI: COLUMBIA BASIN

There are four identified populations in Management Zone VI, which exists mostly in Washington State. Two of these populations, Moses Coulee and Yakima Training Center, are extant populations that were identified and assessed by Garton *et al.* 2011. The additional populations are Crab Creek and Yakama Nation, both of which were addressed with the aid of translocated individuals. Based on information collected at Moses Coulee and Yakima Training Center, Garton *et al.* (2011) predicted a 76.2 percent chance that this population would dip below 200 males in the next 30 years and 86.3 percent chance it would dip below 200 by 2107. Along with the Colorado Plateau, leks in this management zone are the least connected (Knick and Hanser 2011). The PACs likely are large enough to support the current populations and the recovery areas encourage the expansion needed to improve the overall viability. The small size of existing populations and lack of current viability in this management zone means that current management direction (target toward recovery rather than maintenance) is different than in other management zones.

The PACs within this management zone capture redundancy and representation within the management zone, assuming that the protections and management prescriptions area adequate within these areas and they are followed. The PACs were specifically chosen to protect the identified populations. However, because the populations in this management zone are not believed to be viable at this time, the area of protection is larger and designed to include recovery areas which are needed to support a larger, more connected, and hopefully viable population in the future. Based on population viability, it is unlikely that any of the populations in this zone are resilient to threats or disturbances. The order of descending risk is Yakama Nation, Crab Creek, Yakima Training Center, and Moses Coulee.

Moses Coulee

The Moses Coulee population has been maintaining its number for the last 30 years, largely due to the support of farm programs. However, the lower risk of Moses Coulee does not mean that the population is at no risk. This population is at risk. In 2007, 230 males were counted in this population (Garton *et al.* 2011); they estimated an 88 percent probability that the population would dip below 200 males by the year 2037 or close to a 100 percent probability that the population would dip below 200 males by the year 2107. The estimated a 62 percent probability that the population would dip below 20 males by 2107. Despite these dire concerns, the Moses Coulee population of males was estimated to be about 350 in 2012 (Schroeder *et al.* 2012).

Major issues in Moses Coulee are the lack of habitat stability due to the abundant private land, habitat fragmentation, and dependence on farm programs. There is public land managed by the Washington Department of Fish and Wildlife, BLM, Washington and Department of Natural Resources, but the public land is relatively sparse compared to the quantity of private land (Stinson *et al.* 2004). The abundance of private land adds to the management uncertainty. Because of relatively large amounts of enrollment in CRP and State Acres for Wildlife Enhancement (SAFE) programs, there is a great deal of support for sage-grouse in the Moses Coulee area at least for the next decade. Even so, the high degree of fragmentation and 'subsidized' predators (subsidized with road kill, orchards, and nesting and perching structures) increases the overall predation rate.

Yakama Nation

The Yakama Nation population is extremely small with extremely low viability, if any. The area was historically occupied, but the extinction of the endemic population was not precisely documented (Schroeder *et al.* 2000). During 2006-2008 sage-grouse were translocated to the Yakama Nation in an attempt to re-establish a population. Although it is still too early to evaluate success, the results are not promising at this time. The Yakama Nation faces many threats to their sage-grouse population including poor habitat quality, small population size, and lack of connectivity with existing populations, and wild horses. The wild horse population is severe in portions of the Yakama Nation. It is not clear if the Yakama will be able to aggressively deal with the horse issue. On the positive side, the land is owned by the Yakama Nation and the strictly control access. Consequently, they have a great deal of management control as well as interested in recovering a population of sage-grouse on their land. This population is considered high risk.

Crab Creek

The Crab Creek was occupied by sage-grouse until the mid-1980s (Schroeder *et al.* 2000). By the mid-1990s the Washington Department of Wildlife and the BLM had acquired and/or consolidated approximately 50,000 acres in the Crab Creek area. Because sage-grouse were a priority for management on many of these acres and management direction was altered in favor of sage-grouse, it was believed that this area could once again support sage-grouse. Translocations were initiated in 2008 (Schroeder *et al.* 2012). In 2012, the number of males counted on a single lek was 13. Based on survival and productivity, the potential for this population appears promising. However, it is still too early to determine if the re-establishment effort was successful. The primary risk factors for this population include its small size, habitat fragmentation, and the risk of losing acres formerly enrolled in farm programs (CRP and SAFE). This population is considered high risk.

Yakima Training Center

The second most resilient population in this zone is the Yakima Training Center population which is much smaller than Moses Coulee, but is almost entirely public land. Long-term viability is anything but certain. In 2007, 85 males were counted in this population (Garton *et al.* 2012); they estimated a 26 percent probability that the population would dip below 20 males by the year 2037 or 50 percent probability that the population would dip below 20 males by 2107. The number of males counted in 2011 was 72 (Schroeder *et al.* 2012). The use of the Yakima Training Center for military training activities and the risk of fire have reduced the overall suitability of the habitat supporting this population. A substantial amount of the sage-grouse habitat on the area has been harmed directly and indirectly military training activities, particularly due to wildfires. Despite efforts to manage wildfire risks, wildfires have continued to reduce the quality of habitat in the population. Other key factors in this population are two interstate highways (I 82 and I 90) which border the population on north and west side, powerlines which border the population on the north, west, and south sides, the Columbia River Valley which is natural but reduces movement on the east side, and wind development on the north side. The cumulative effect of these factors is that the population is constricted with little opportunity for expansion. On the positive side, the population occupies and area dominated by public land. This population is considered high risk.

MANAGEMENT ZONE VII: COLORADO PLATEAU

This management zone contains two populations; Parachute-Piceance Basin and Meeker-White River Colorado. The designated priority areas for conservation appear to capture redundancy and representation. Priority habitats are well mapped and include all high use habitat (which includes breeding, summer, and winter habitat within 4 miles of all known leks) and linkage zones to Management Zone 2 to the north. There is no known connectivity with Utah

(Management Zone 3 to the west) due to natural habitat fragmentation and large areas of non-habitat.

Parachute-Piceance-Roan

The Parachute-Piceance-Roan Basin population appears to be captured within priority areas for conservation, and representation appears to be captured adequately. Priority areas for conservation capture 60 percent of the occupied range in this population and also include 100 percent of all known active leks and all habitats that were modeled "high probability of use" within four miles of a lek that has been active in the last 10 years. Redundancy is not captured within this population because it is a relatively small (three year running average number of males is 93) and somewhat isolated. This population is on the very southern edge of the species range. There is some potential for connectivity to the north to the Wyoming Basin population in Management Zone 2. Linkage habitats have been included in mapping efforts. Representation and redundancy are at risk within this population due to its small size, energy development and the associated infrastructure, especially road development. Pinyon-juniper encroachment is also an issue. The Parachute-Piceance-Roan population appears to have some resiliency. The population has been monitored since 2005 and appears to be fluctuating similar to other larger populations in the state. A large majority of PACs are privately owned, mostly by energy companies. Energy and mineral development is the highest ranked threat to sage-grouse in this area. Advances in drilling technology and rapid natural gas demand and subsequent rising prices have led to a significant increase in natural gas drilling activity. Road and infrastructure are also ranked high as they are closely related to energy production. Historic habitat has been lost and fragmented also by pinyon-juniper encroachment. This population is considered to be at high risk.

Meeker-White River Colorado

This population is located just northeast of Parachute-Piceance-Roan Basin. There is no redundancy and little representation in the Meeker-White River population (three-year running average high male count is six birds). Priority areas for conservation capture 27 percent of the occupied range in this population and include the only known active lek. All habitats modeled "high probability of use" and within four miles of any lek (active in the last 10 years) are within priority habitat. Representation and redundancy are at risk within this population due to its small size, proximity to an urbanized setting and, thus, housing development and associated infrastructure and agriculture conversion. This is a very small population located near the town of Meeker and consists of only one active lek that was discovered in 2004, and strutting male counts have been on a steady decline since (e.g., from a high of 30 males in 2004 to six males in 2012). Most of the occupied habitat is privately owned (90 percent) and is in two disconnected patches of habitat, separated by the White River. One of the patches remains unfragmented. The other patch is located where housing development will primarily occur. Meeker-White River has lost resiliency. The population has been monitored since 2004 and the population has been in a steady decline from 30 males to the current six males. Housing development is increasing mainly due to energy development in nearby counties. A large part of the habitat was converted to agriculture in the 1960's, which is likely a primary reason why the population went into decline. A current issue is that some of the lands in pasture and CRP land may now be converted back to crop lands. This population is considered to be at high risk.

BI-STATE DPS

The Bi-State Distinct Population Segment (Bi-State DPS) is geographically and genetically isolated from other populations of greater sage-grouse (Oyler McCance *et al.* 2005, Benedict *et al.* 2003). Four populations are identified in the Bi-State DPS, including: Pine Nut, North of Mono Lake, South of Mono Lake, and the White Mountains. These populations are delineated based on a fair degree of geographic and genetic isolation within the overall Bi-State DPS. Within the Bi-State, all occupied habitat is considered PAC. Two core populations exist to the north and south of Mono Lake, with small peripheral populations in the Pine Nut Range to the north and White Mountains to the south. Garton *et al.* (2011) indicate that long-term persistence is questionable for both core populations with a high probability of dropping below effective population sizes of 50 birds in the next 100 years (100 percent for North Mono and 81.5 percent for South Mono). However, probability of dropping below effective population sizes of 50 birds is low in the next 30 years (15.4 percent for North Mono and 0.1 percent for South Mono. The Bi-State DPS has grown consistently each year from 2008–2012 to the highest population size on record, presumably in response to a trend in higher precipitation and favorable range conditions. Relatively large population increases have been seen in the core populations to the north and south of Mono Lake that have multiple well-connected leks, while peripheral populations have not seen these population increases. The Bi-State DPS is still represented in most of the known historic distribution, but threatened by small and isolated populations on the periphery of the range. Genetic diversity remains high in most of the Bi-State DPS, with emerging evidence that representation has been lost in some areas by population reduction and some loss of genetic diversity.

North Mono Lake

The population to the north of Mono Lake consists of a central stronghold located in the Bodie Hills, CA, and several additional peripheral populations in CA and NV that vary in size and degree of isolation. The Bodie Hills population has grown in recent years to be the largest and most connected population in the Bi-State, with more than 500 males counted on leks in 2012. The Bodie Hills breeding complex has about 9 to 11 core leks, ranging from about 100-500 males counted over the past 20 years. The Bodie Hills breeding complex appears to be best connected with the Aurora, Rough Creek and Nine Mile Flat area within the Mount Grant PMU in Nevada. This area, plus Mount Grant proper in the Wassuk Range contains eight active leks. The Fales area in California, consisting of two known leks at Wheeler Flat and Burcham Flat on the northwestern edge of this population, is largely isolated from Bodie, but probably has some connectivity to another small population at Jackass Spring along the border and Desert Creek/Sweetwater Flat in NV. The Fales population was much larger prior to the early 1980's and has experienced the greatest population declines in California, with less than 100 males counted on leks in 2012. The core population to the north of Mono Lake in total appears to be fairly resistant but individual subpopulations much less so. While the population remains relatively stable, the size and geographical extent is moderately small and the degree of historic impacts has not been severe. Although there is good resistance in the core of this population, additional threats should be avoided in both the core and peripheral areas. The North Mono Lake population is the largest population in the Bi-State and least isolated, and is potentially at risk because of periodic fluctuations in population size, and multiple threats to the population.

South Mono Lake

The population to the south of Mono Lake consists of a central stronghold located in Long Valley, CA. The Long Valley and Bodie Hills populations are considered the two main core populations in the Bi-State DPS. Similar to Bodie, the Long Valley population has grown in recent years, with more than 400 males counted on leks in 2012. Similar to the Bodie Hills, the Long Valley breeding complex contains about 9-11 core leks, with about 150-400 males counted over the past 20 years. One additional breeding population located at Parker Creek in CA is considered isolated from Long Valley and only known to contain one lek. The Long Valley breeding complex remains relatively stable and resistance to ongoing impacts is generally good. As with the North Mono population, however, this breeding complex is not overly large. The Long Valley population is probably more vulnerable than Bodie because it is considered isolated from other Bi-State populations and seasonal habitats are limited to a relatively small area. Therefore, this population could be severely impacted by catastrophic events, and further cumulative threats should be avoided. The Parker population is probably fewer than 100 estimated birds total and lacks resistance. The South Mono Lake is currently relatively large population, but is potentially at risk because of isolation, periodic fluctuations in population size, and multiple threats to the population.

Pine Nut

The Pine Nut population is the smallest and most threatened population in the Bi-State DPS. The population consists of one consistently active lek, although there is indication that additional sites may be present and there is some connectivity to the population to the north of Mono Lake. The long-term average male attendance is approximately 14 males over the past 11 years. The population appears predisposed to environmental vagaries in the form of wildfire and drought as well as additional anthropogenic stressors that have and continue to influence the population. These conditions have resulted in a population that is largely nonresistant to additional impacts. The Pine Nut population is classified as high risk because of very low population size and relatively high level of threats.

White Mountains

The population in the White Mountains is not well understood because of difficulty in accessing the area to conduct lek surveys. However, at least one lek is known to exist at Chiatovich Flat in California and 2 recently discovered leks are known to exist in NV. As with the other Bi-State breeding populations, sage-grouse in the White Mountains are probably mostly threatened by small population size and are therefore vulnerable to catastrophic events. However, this population, located in high elevation habitats on the extreme southwest of the species range, has probably always been small and faces the fewest threats in the Bi-State DPS. The White Mountains are classified as potential risk because of the aforementioned uncertainty regarding population size, but has the least land use threats in the Bi-State DPS.

APPENDIX B—POLICY FOR THE EVALUATION OF CONSERVATION EFFORTS WHEN MAKING LISTING DECISIONS

preferred the rulemaking petition. The coordinates for Channel 287C3 at Alamo are 32–19–29 North Latitude and 82–43–23 West Longitude. This allotment has a site restriction of 20.4 kilometers (12.7 miles) north of Alamo.

DATES: Effective April 28, 2003.

FOR FURTHER INFORMATION CONTACT: R. Barthen Gorman, Media Bureau, (202) 418–2180.

SUPPLEMENTARY INFORMATION: This is a synopsis of the Commission's Report and Order, MM Docket No. 01–111, adopted March 12, 2003, and released March 14, 2003. The full text of this Commission decision is available for inspection and copying during normal business hours in the FCC's Reference Information Center at Portals II, 445 12th Street, SW., Room CY–A257, Washington, DC, 20554. The document may also be purchased from the Commission's duplicating contractor, Qualex International, Portals II, 445 12th Street, SW., Room CY–B402, Washington, DC, 20554, telephone 202 863–2893. facsimile 202 863–2898, or via e-mail *qualexint@aol.com.*

List of Subjects in 47 CFR Part 73

Radio, Radio broadcasting.

■ Part 73 of Title 47 of the Code of Federal Regulations is amended as follows:

PART 73—RADIO BROADCAST SERVICES

■ 1. The authority citation for Part 73 reads as follows:

Authority: 47 U.S.C. 154, 303, 334 and 336.

§ 73.202 [Amended]

■ 2. Section 73.202(b), the Table of FM Allotments under Georgia, is amended by adding Alamo, Channel 287C3.

Federal Communications Commission.

John A. Karousos,
Assistant Chief, Audio Division Media Bureau.

[FR Doc. 03–7470 Filed 3–27–03; 8:45 am]
BILLING CODE 6712–01–P

FEDERAL COMMUNICATIONS COMMISSION

47 CFR Part 73

[DA 03–629; MB Docket No. 02–120; RM–10442]

Radio Broadcasting Services; Owen, Wisconsin

AGENCY: Federal Communications Commission.

ACTION: Final rule.

SUMMARY: The Audio Division, at the request of Starboard Broadcasting, Inc.,

allots Channel 242C3 at Owen, Wisconsin, as the community's first local FM service. Channel 242C3 can be allotted to Owen, Wisconsin, in compliance with the Commission's minimum distance separation requirements with a site restriction of 12.9 km (8.0 miles) northeast of Owen. The coordinates for Channel 242C3 at Owen, Wisconsin, are 45–03–08 North Latitude and 90–29–21 West Longitude. A filing window for Channel 242C3 at Owen, WI, will not be opened at this time. Instead, the issue of opening this allotment for auction will be addressed by the Commission in a subsequent Order.

DATES: Effective April 28, 2003.

FOR FURTHER INFORMATION CONTACT: Deborah Dupont, Media Bureau, (202) 418–2180.

SUPPLEMENTARY INFORMATION: This is a synopsis of the Commission's Report and Order, MB Docket No. 02–120, adopted March 12, 2003, and released March 14, 2003. The full text of this Commission decision is available for inspection and copying during normal business hours in the FCC Information Center, Portals II, 445 12th Street, SW., Room CY–A257, Washington, DC 20554. The complete text of this decision may also be purchased from the Commission's duplicating contractor, Qualex International, Portals II, 445 12th Street, SW., Room CY–B402, Washington, DC, 20554, (202) 863–2893, facsimile (202) 863–2898, or via e-mail *qualexint@aol.com.*

List of Subjects in 47 CFR Part 73

Radio, Radio broadcasting.

■ Part 73 of title 47 of the Code of Federal Regulations is amended as follows:

PART 73—RADIO BROADCAST SERVICES

■ 1. The authority citation for part 73 continues to read as follows:

Authority: 47 U.S.C. 154, 303, 334 and 336.

§ 73.202 [Amended]

■ 2. Section 73.202(b), the Table of FM Allotments under Wisconsin, is amended by adding Owen, Channel 242C3.

Federal Communications Commission.

John A. Karousos,
Assistant Chief, Audio Division, Media Bureau.

[FR Doc. 03–7472 Filed 3–27–03; 8:45 am]
BILLING CODE 6712–01–P

DEPARTMENT OF THE INTERIOR

Fish and Wildlife Service

DEPARTMENT OF COMMERCE

National Oceanic and Atmospheric Administration

50 CFR Chapter IV

[Docket No. 000214043–2227–02; I.D. 011603A]

RIN 1018–AF55, 0648–XA48

Policy for Evaluation of Conservation Efforts When Making Listing Decisions

AGENCIES: Fish and Wildlife Service, Interior; National Marine Fisheries Service, NOAA, Commerce.

ACTION: Announcement of final policy.

SUMMARY: We, the Fish and Wildlife Service (FWS) and the National Marine Fisheries Service (NMFS) (the Services), announce a final policy for the evaluation of conservation efforts when making listing decisions (PECE) under the Endangered Species Act of 1973, as amended (Act). While the Act requires us to take into account all conservation efforts being made to protect a species, the policy identifies criteria we will use in determining whether formalized conservation efforts that have yet to be implemented or to show effectiveness contribute to making listing a species as threatened or endangered unnecessary. The policy applies to conservation efforts identified in conservation agreements, conservation plans, management plans, or similar documents developed by Federal agencies, State and local governments, Tribal governments, businesses, organizations, and individuals.

DATES: This policy is effective April 28, 2003.

ADDRESSES: Chief, Division of Conservation and Classification, U.S. Fish and Wildlife Service, 4401 North Fairfax Drive, Arlington, VA 22203 (Telephone 703/358–2171, Facsimile 703/358–1735); or Chief, Endangered Species Division, National Marine Fisheries Service, Office of Protected Resources, 1315 East-West Highway, Silver Spring, MD 20910 (Telephone 301/713–1401, Facsimile 301/713–0376).

FOR FURTHER INFORMATION CONTACT: Chris Nolin, Chief, Division of Conservation and Classification, U.S. Fish and Wildlife Service at the above address, telephone 703/358–2171 or facsimile 703/358–1735, or Margaret Lorenz, Endangered Species Division, National Marine Fisheries Service at the above address, telephone 301/713–1401 or facsimile 301/713–0376.

SUPPLEMENTARY INFORMATION:

Background

This policy provides direction to Service personnel in determining how to consider a conservation agreement when making a decision on whether a species warrants listing under the Act. It also provides information to the groups interested in developing agreements or plans that would contribute to making it unnecessary for the Services to list a species under the Act.

On June 13, 2000, we published in the **Federal Register** (65 FR 37102) a draft policy for evaluating conservation efforts that have not yet been implemented or have not yet demonstrated effectiveness when making listing decisions under the Act. The policy establishes two basic criteria: (1) The certainty that the conservation efforts will be implemented and (2) the certainty that the efforts will be effective. The policy provides specific factors under these two basic criteria that we will use to direct our analysis of the conservation effort. At the time of making listing determinations, we will evaluate formalized conservation efforts (i.e., conservation efforts identified in a conservation agreement, conservation plan, management plan, or similar document) to determine if the conservation effort provides certainty of implementation and effectiveness and, thereby, improves the status, as defined by the Act, of the species such that it does not meet the Act's definition of a threatened or endangered species.

When we evaluate the certainty of whether the formalized conservation effort will be implemented, we will consider the following: Do we have a high level of certainty that the resources necessary to carry out the conservation effort are available? Do the parties to the conservation effort have the authority to carry it out? Are the regulatory or procedural mechanisms in place to carry out the efforts? And is there a schedule for completing and evaluating the efforts? If the conservation effort relies on voluntary participation, we will evaluate whether the incentives that are included in the conservation effort will ensure the level of participation necessary to carry out the conservation effort. We will also evaluate the certainty that the conservation effort will be effective. In making this evaluation, we will consider the following: Does the effort describe the nature and extent of the threats to the species to be addressed and how these threats are reduced by

the conservation effort? Does the effort establish specific conservation objectives? Does the effort identify the appropriate steps to reduce threats to the species? And does the effort include quantifiable performance measures to monitor for both compliance and effectiveness? Overall, we need to be certain that the formalized conservation effort improves the status of the species at the time we make a listing determination.

This policy is important because it gives us a consistent set of criteria to evaluate formalized conservation efforts. For states and other entities that are developing agreements or plans, this policy informs them of the criteria we will use in evaluating formalized conservation efforts when making listing decisions, and thereby guides States and other entities that wish to develop formalized conservation efforts that may contribute to making listing unnecessary.

In the notice of the draft policy, we specifically requested comments on the criteria that we would use to evaluate the certainty that a formalized conservation effort will be implemented. Also, we requested comments on the timing of the development of conservation agreements or plans. We have learned that timing is the most critical element when developing a successful conservation agreement or plan. Encouraging and facilitating early development of conservation agreements or plans is an important objective of this policy. Last-minute agreements (i.e., those that are developed just before or after a species is proposed for listing) often have little chance of affecting the outcome of a listing decision. Once a species is proposed for listing under the Act, we may have insufficient time to include consideration of a newly developed conservation plan in the public notice and comment process and still meet our statutory deadlines. Last-minute efforts are also less likely to be able to demonstrate that they will be implemented and effective in reducing or removing threats to the species. In addition, there are circumstances in which the threats to a species are so imminent and/or complex that it will be almost impossible to develop an agreement or plan that includes conservation efforts that will result in making the listing unnecessary. Accordingly, we encourage the early development of formalized conservation efforts before the threats become too extreme and imminent and when there is greater flexibility in sufficiently improving a species' status to the point

where listing the species as threatened or endangered is unnecessary.

Summary of Comments and Recommendations

In response to our request for comments on the draft policy, we received letters from 44 entities. Thirty-five were in support of the policy and nine were against. We reviewed all comments received and have incorporated accepted suggestions or clarifications into the final policy text. Because most of these letters included similar comments (several were form letters) we grouped the comments according to issues. The following is a summary of the relevant comments and our responses. We also received comments that were not relevant to the policy and, therefore, outside the policy's scope. We responded to some of these comments where doing so would clarify the process for determining whether a species is endangered or threatened (the listing process) or clarify the nature of conservation plans, agreements, and efforts.

Policy Scope Issues

Issue 1: Many commenters felt that this policy should also apply to downlisting species from endangered to threatened status and delisting actions, or else parties to an agreement where the final decision is to list the species would not have any incentives to take action on a listed species until a recovery plan is developed. In addition, one commenter suggested that the policy scope should be expanded to include the process of designating critical habitat.

Response 1: We believe that the immediate need is to develop criteria that will guide consistent and predictable evaluation of conservation efforts at the time of a listing determination. We may consider such a policy for downlisting or delisting actions in the future. However, we note that a recovery plan is the appropriate vehicle to provide guidance on actions necessary to delist a species. Also, we may consider developing a similar policy for critical habitat designations.

Issue 2: Two commenters stated that our estimates of time needed to develop, implement, monitor, and report on conservation efforts are underestimated.

Response 2: We agree that our original estimates were too low. We have increased our estimate to an average of 2,500 person-hours to complete a conservation agreement (with a range of 1,000 to 4,000 person-hours). We also increased our estimate of the average number of person-hours to conduct monitoring and to prepare a report to

320 and 80 hours, respectively. We expect the amount of time will vary depending on several factors including, but not limited to, the number of species addressed, amount of biological information available on the species, and the complexity of the threats. Therefore, we have provided an average to assist interested parties in their planning efforts.

Issue 3: One commenter questioned whether we would evaluate proposed agreements or plans using the stated criteria automatically or only upon request. The commenter also questioned whether we will consider agreements or plans that we previously determined were not sufficient to prevent the need for listing in combination with "new" proposed agreements or plans when we evaluate whether to list a species.

Response 3: If a listing proposal is under review, we will consider any conservation effort. We will evaluate the status of the species in the context of all factors that affect the species' risk of extinction, including all known conservation efforts whether planned, under way, or fully implemented. However, for formalized conservation efforts not fully implemented, or where the results have not been demonstrated, we will consider the PECE criteria in our evaluation of whether, and to what extent, the formalized conservation efforts affect the species' status under the Act.

Issue 4: One commenter asked the length of time for which a plan is approved.

Response 4: The PECE is not a plan-approval process, nor does it establish an alternative to listing. PECE outlines the criteria we will consider when evaluating formalized conservation efforts that have not yet been fully implemented or do not yet have a record of effectiveness at the time we make a listing decision. Should the status of a species decline after we make a decision not to list this species, we would need to reassess our listing decision. For example, there may be situations where the parties to a plan or agreement meet their commitments, but unexpected and/or increased threats (e.g., disease) may occur that threaten the species' status and make it necessary to list the species.

Issue 5: One commenter asked if the "new information" reopener is operative at any time.

Response 5: Yes, because section 4(b)(1) of the Act requires us to use the best available scientific and commercial data whenever making decisions during the listing process. In making a decision whether to list a species, we will take into account all available information,

including new information regarding formalized conservation efforts. If we receive new information on a formalized conservation effort that has not yet been implemented or not yet demonstrated effectiveness prior to making a listing decision, we will evaluate the conservation effort in the context of the PECE criteria. If we receive new information on such an effort after we have decided to list a species, then we will consider this new information along with other measures that reduce threats to the species and may use this information in downlisting the species from endangered to threatened status or delisting. However, PECE will not control our analysis of the downlisting of the species.

Issue 6: One commenter stated that it is unrealistic and unreasonable to expect agreements to be in place at the time the conservation effort is evaluated. In addition, the commenter stated that it is particularly unrealistic and unreasonable to expect that conservation agreements or plans be submitted within 60 days of publication of a proposed rule.

Response 6: We strongly encourage parties to initiate formalized conservation efforts prior to publication of a proposal to list a species under the Act. If a formalized conservation effort is submitted during the public comment period for a proposed rule, and may be significant to the listing decision, then we may extend or reopen the comment period to allow time for comment on the new conservation effort. However, we can extend the public comment period only if doing so does not prevent us from completing the final listing action within the statutory timeframe.

Issue 7: One commenter stated that most existing conservation agreements are ineffective, and furthermore that we are unable to determine their effectiveness for several years.

Response 7: We agree that it could take several years for some conservation efforts to demonstrate results. However, the PECE criteria provide the framework for us to evaluate the likely effectiveness of such formalized conservation efforts. Some existing conservation efforts have proven to be very effective and have justifiably influenced our listing decisions.

Issue 8: Several commenters stated that funds are better spent to list species, designate critical habitat, and implement recovery efforts rather than to develop conservation agreements.

Response 8: Conservation agreements can be seen as early recovery efforts. Early conservation efforts to improve the status of a species before listing is necessary may cost less than if the

species' status has already been reduced to the point where it needs to be listed. Early conservation of candidate species can reduce threats and stabilize or increase populations sufficiently to allow us to use our resources for species in greater need of the Act's protective measures.

Issue 9: Some commenters questioned the 14 conservation agreements that we cited which contributed to making listing the covered species as threatened or endangered unnecessary. Commenters requested information on each plan to better allow the public to evaluate the adequacy of the agreements.

Response 9: We referenced the 14 conservation agreements in the Paperwork Reduction Act section of the draft policy and used them solely to estimate the information collection and recordkeeping burden that would result from our draft policy if it were made final. Therefore, we do not recommend using these to comment on the new policy.

Biological Issues

Issue 10: One commenter questioned our method for evaluating a conservation plan that addresses only a portion of a species' range.

Response 10: Using the PECE criteria, we will evaluate all formalized conservation efforts that have yet to be implemented or have yet to demonstrate results at the time we make our listing decision. This is true for efforts that are applicable to all or only a portion of the species' range. The PECE does not set standards for how much conservation is needed to make listing unnecessary. The significance of plans that address only a portion of a species' range will be evaluated in the context of the species' overall status. While a formalized conservation effort may be effective in reducing or removing threats in a portion of the species' range, that may or may not be sufficient to remove the need to list the species as threatened or endangered. In some cases, the conservation effort may lead to a determination that a species warrants threatened status rather than endangered.

In addition, parties may have entered into agreements to obtain assurances that no additional commitments or restrictions will be required if the species is listed. A landowner or other non-Federal entity can enter into a Candidate Conservation Agreement with Assurances (CCAA) (64 FR 32726, June 17, 1999), which are formal agreements between us and one or more non-Federal parties that address the conservation needs of proposed or candidate species, or species likely to become candidates. These agreements provide assurances to non-Federal property owners who voluntarily agree to manage their lands or waters to remove threats to candidate or proposed species, or to species likely to become candidates. The assurances are authorized under the CCAA regulations (50 CFR 17. 22(d)(5) and 17.32(d)(5)) and provide non-Federal property owners assurances that their conservation efforts will not result in future regulatory obligations in excess of those they agree to at the time they enter into the Agreement. Should the species eventually be listed under the Act, landowners will not be subjected to increased property use restrictions as long as they conform to the terms of the agreement. While one of these agreements may not remove the need to list, several such agreements, covering a large portion of the species' range, may.

Issue 11: Several commenters suggested that the Services should consider conservation efforts developed for species other than the species for which a listing decision is being made when the species have similar biological requirements and the conservation effort addresses protection of habitat of the species for which a listing decision is being made.

Response 11: We agree. When a decision whether or not to list a species is being made, we will consider all conservation efforts that reduce or remove threats to the species under review, including conservation efforts developed for other species. However, for all formalized conservation efforts that have not yet been implemented or have yet to demonstrate results, we will use the PECE criteria to evaluate the conservation effort for certainty of implementation and effectiveness for the species subject to the listing decision.

Issue 12: One commenter stated the "biology/natural history" of the species should be adequately known and explained in order to evaluate the effectiveness of the effort.

Response 12: When we consider the elements under the effectiveness criterion, we will evaluate whether the formalized conservation effort incorporates the best available information on the species' biology and natural history. However, due to variation in the amount of information available about different species and the threats to their existence, the level of information necessary to provide a high level of certainty that the effort will be effective will vary.

We believe it is important, however, to start conservation efforts as early as

possible even if complete biological information is lacking. Regardless of the extent of biological information we have about a species, there will almost always be some uncertainty about threats and the most effective mechanisms for improving the status of a species. We will include the extent of gaps in the available information in our evaluation of the level of certainty that the formalized conservation effort will be effective. One method of addressing uncertainty and accommodating new information is the use of monitoring and the application of adaptive management principles. The PECE criteria note that describing the threats and how those threats will be removed, including the use of monitoring and adaptive management principles, as appropriate, is critical to determining that a conservation effort that has yet to demonstrate results has reduced or removed a particular threat to a species.

Issue 13: Several commenters suggested that affected party(ies) should work with the Services to identify species that will be proposed for listing in the near future to help concentrate and direct efforts to those species that most warrant the protection, and help make the party(ies) aware of when and what actions should be taken to help conserve species in need.

Response 13: We do identify species in need of protection. The FWS publishes a Candidate Notice of Review (CNOR) in which the FWS identifies those species of plants and animals for which they have sufficient information on the species' biological status and threats to propose them as endangered or threatened under the Act, but for which development of a proposed listing regulation is precluded by other higher priority listing activities. NMFS, which has jurisdiction over marine species and some anadromous species, defines candidate species more broadly to include species whose status is of concern but more information is needed before they can be proposed for listing. NMFS candidate species can be found on their web site at *http:// www.nmfs.noaa.gov.* The FWS's CNOR is published in the **Federal Register** and can also be found on their web site at *http://endangered.fws.gov.*

We agree that it is important to start developing and implementing conservation efforts and coordinating those efforts with us as early as possible. Early conservation helps preserve management options, minimizes the cost of reducing threats to a species, and reduces the potential for land use restrictions in the future. Addressing the needs of species before the regulatory protections associated with listing

under the Act come into play often allows greater management flexibility in the actions necessary to stabilize or restore these species and their habitats. Early implementation of conservation efforts may reduce the risk of extinction for some species, thus eliminating the need for them to be listed as threatened or endangered.

Issue 14: One commenter stated that requiring an implementation schedule/timeline for conservation objectives is not feasible when baseline data on a species is poorly understood. The policy should recognize that variation in patterns of species distribution and land ownership will cause variation in the difficulty of developing conservation efforts. Thus, some conservation efforts should be allotted more time for their completion.

Response 14: Biological uncertainty is a common feature of any conservation effort. Nevertheless, some conservation actions can proceed even when information on the species is incomplete. Implementation schedules are an important element of all formalized conservation planning efforts (e.g., recovery plans). The implementation schedule identified in PECE criterion A.8. establishes a timeframe with incremental completion dates for specific tasks. In light of the information gaps that may exist for some species or actions, schedules for completing certain tasks may require revision in response to new information, changing circumstances, and the application of adaptive management principles. Including an implementation schedule in a formalized conservation effort is critical to determining that the effort will be implemented and effective and has improved the status of the species under the Act at the time we make our listing determination.

We acknowledge that the amount of time required to develop and implement formalized conservation efforts will vary. Therefore, we encourage early development and implementation of conservation efforts for species that have not yet become candidates for listing and for those species that are already candidates. This policy does not dictate timeframes for completing conservation efforts. However, the Act mandates specific timeframes for many listing decisions, and we cannot delay final listing actions to allow for the development and signing of a conservation agreement or plan. We and participants must also acknowledge that, for species that are poorly known, or whose threats are not well understood, it is unlikely that conservation efforts that have not been implemented or that have yet to yield results will have improved the status of the species sufficiently to play a significant role in the listing decision.

Issue 15: One commenter stated that the Services, when evaluating the certainty of conservation efforts while making listing decisions, should factor into the analysis the Services' ability to open or reopen the listing process at any time, and to list the species on an emergency basis if necessary.

Response 15: We will initiate or revisit a listing decision if information indicates that doing so is warranted, and on an emergency basis if there is an imminent threat to the species' well-being. However, we do not make any listing determinations based on our ability to change our decisions. We base our listing decisions on the status of the species at that time, not on some time in the future.

Criteria Issues

Issue 16: Several commenters requested that we further explain the criteria for both implementation and effectiveness. The commenters claim that our criteria are too vague and are subject to interpretation by the Services. One commenter said that, by stating "this list should not be considered comprehensive evaluation criteria," the policy allows the Services to consider criteria not addressed in the agreement, and allows for too much leeway for the Services to reject conservation efforts of an agreement, even if all criteria listed in the draft policy are satisfied.

Response 16: PECE establishes a set of criteria for us to consider when evaluating formalized conservation efforts that have not yet been implemented or have not yet demonstrated effectiveness to determine if the efforts have improved the status of the species. At the time of the listing decision, we must find, with minimal uncertainty, that a particular formalized conservation effort will be implemented and will be effective, in order to find that the effort has positively affected the conservation status of a species. Meeting these criteria does not create an approval process. Some conservation efforts will address these criteria more thoroughly than others. Because, in part, circumstances vary greatly among species, we must evaluate all conservation efforts on a case-by-case basis at the time of listing, taking into account any and all factors relevant to whether the conservation effort will be implemented and effective.

Similarly, the list of criteria is not comprehensive because the conservation needs of species will vary greatly and depend on species-specific, habitat-specific, location-specific, and action-specific factors. Because conservation needs vary, it is not possible to state all of the factors that might determine the ultimate effectiveness of formalized conservation efforts. The species-specific circumstances will also determine the amount of information necessary to satisfy these criteria. Evaluating the certainty of the effectiveness of a formalized conservation effort necessarily includes an evaluation of the technical adequacy of the effort. For example, the effectiveness of creating a wetland for species conservation will depend on soil texture, hydrology, water chemistry, and other factors. Listing all of the factors that we would appropriately consider in evaluations of technical adequacy is not possible.

Issue 17: One commenter suggested that we consider conservation plans in the development stage rather than waiting until finalized due to the possible benefits that may result from initial efforts.

Response 17: Plans that have not been finalized and, therefore, do not conform to the PECE criteria, may have some conservation value for the species. For example, in the process of developing a plan, participants and the public may become more informed about the species and its conservation needs. We will consider any benefits to a species that have accrued prior to the completion of an agreement or plan in our listing decision, under section 4(b)(1)(A) of the Act. However, the mere existence of a planning process does not provide sufficient certainty to actually improve the status of a species. The criteria of PECE set a rigorous standard for analysis and assure a high level of certainty associated with formalized conservation efforts that have not been implemented, or have yet to yield results, in order to determine that the status of the species has improved.

We encourage parties to involve the appropriate Service during the development stage of all conservation plans, whether or not they are finalized prior to a listing decision. Sharing of the best available information can lead to developing better agreements. In the event that the focus species is listed, these planning efforts can be utilized as the basis for development of Safe Harbor Agreements or Habitat Conservation Plans, through which we can permit incidental take under Section 10(a) of the Act, or provide a basis for a recovery plan.

Issue 18: Several commenters stated that the policy should provide more sufficient, clear criteria by which the implementation and effectiveness of conservation efforts is monitored and assessed. One commenter also suggested that we require a specific reporting format to help show effectiveness of conservation efforts.

Response 18: When evaluating formalized conservation efforts under PECE, we will consider whether the effort contains provisions for monitoring and reporting implementation and effectiveness results (see criterion B.5).

Regarding a standard reporting format, the nature of the formalized conservation efforts we evaluate will probably vary a great deal. Efforts may range from complex to single-threat approaches. Therefore, for us to adopt a one-size-fits-all approach to report on monitoring efforts and results would be inappropriate.

Issue 19: One commenter stated that PECE is too demanding with respect to identification and commitment of resources "up-front," and that these strict requirements and commitments on conservation efforts harm the voluntary nature of agreements.

Response 19: Addressing the resources necessary to carry out a conservation effort is central to establishing certainty of plan implementation and effectiveness. Accordingly, we believe that PECE must establish a minimum standard to assure certainty of implementation and effectiveness. This certainty is necessary in determining whether the conservation effort has improved the status of species.

It is our intention and belief that the PECE criteria will actually increase the voluntary participation in conservation agreements by increasing the likelihood that parties' voluntary efforts and commitments that have yet to be implemented or have yet to demonstrate results will play a role in a listing decision.

Issues Related to Specific Changes

Several commenters recommended specific changes to the evaluation criteria. The recommended additions in language to the criteria are italicized and deletions are shown in strikeout to help the reader identify the proposed changes.

Issue 20: Commenters stated that there is potential confusion between evaluation criteria A.2. (authority) and A.3.(authorization) as they believed some Service staff may have difficulty distinguishing between an "authority," and an "authorization." To help eliminate this potential confusion, commenters requested that criterion A.2. be changed to read: "the legal authority of the party(ies) to the agreement or plan to implement the conservation effort and the legal procedural requirements necessary to implement the effort are described." They also requested that we change criterion A.3. to read: The legal requirements (e.g. permits, environmental review documents) necessary to implement the conservation effort are identified, and an explanation of how the party(ies) to the agreement or plan that will implement the effort will fulfill these requirements is provided."

Response 20: We agree with adding the word "legal" and also have incorporated additional language and separated this criterion (former criterion A.2) into two criteria (A.2. and A.3.). Evaluation Criterion A.2. now reads, "The legal authority of the party(ies) to the agreement or plan to implement the formalized conservation effort, and the commitment to proceed with the conservation effort are described." New evaluation Criterion A.3. reads, "The legal procedural requirements necessary to implement the effort are described, and information is provided indicating that fulfillment of these requirements does not preclude commitment to the effort." In making these changes, we recognize that there may be overlap between new criterion A.3. and the criterion on authorizations (now A.4.), but our intent is to separate a criterion on procedural requirements from substantive authorizations (e.g. permits). We believe that we need to specifically determine that the parties to the agreement will obtain the necessary authorizations. We also recognize that parties may not be able to commit to some conservation efforts until they have fulfilled procedural requirements (e.g. under the National Environmental Policy Act) since some laws preclude commitment to a specific action until certain procedures are completed. Additionally, in creating a new criterion A.3., we find it unnecessary to incorporate the suggested changes to old A.3. (now A.4.).

Issue 21: Commenters requested the following change to Criterion A.4. (now Criterion A.5.): "The level of voluntary participation (e.g., permission to enter private land or other contributions by private landowners) necessary to implement the conservation effort is identified, and an explanation of how the party(ies) to the agreement or plan that will implement the conservation effort will obtain that level of voluntary participation is provided (e.g., an explanation of why incentives to be provided are expected to result in the necessary level of voluntary participation)".

Response 21: We do not believe that including "an explanation of how the

party(ies) * * * will obtain that level of voluntary participation * * *" will provide us with enough information in order to determine that necessary voluntary participation will, in fact, be obtained. Evaluation Criterion A.5. (formerly A.4.) now reads: "The type and level of voluntary participation (e.g., number of landowners allowing entry to their land, or number of participants agreeing to change timber management practices and acreage involved) necessary to implement the conservation effort is identified, and a high level of certainty is provided that the party(ies) to the agreement or plan that will implement the conservation effort will obtain that level of voluntary participation (e.g., an explanation of how incentives to be provided will result in the necessary level of voluntary participation)."

Issue 22: Commenters suggested that Evaluation Criterion A.5. (now criterion A.6.) be changed to read as "Any statutory or regulatory deficiency or barrier to implementation of the conservation effort is identified and an explanation of how the party(ies) to the agreement or plan that will implement the effort will resolve the deficiency or barriers is provided."

Response 22: We do not agree with the suggested language change. We believe that all regulatory mechanisms, including statutory authorities, must be in place to ensure a high level of certainty that the conservation effort will be implemented.

Issue 23: The suggested change to Evaluation Criterion A.6. (now A.7.) is "A fiscal schedule and plan is provided for the conservation effort, including a description of the obligations of party(ies) to the agreement or plan that will implement the conservation effort, and an explanation of how they will obtain the necessary funding is provided."

Response 23: We do not agree with the suggested language change since we believe that there must be a high level of certainty that the party(ies) will obtain the necessary funding to implement the effort. While we agree that including a fiscal schedule, a description of the obligations of the party(ies), and an explanation of how they will obtain the funding is important, this information, by itself, does not provide enough certainty for us to consider a formalized conservation effort that has not yet been implemented as contributing to a listing decision. Also see our response to Issue 41.

Issue 24: One commenter suggested that the Services should consider an incremental approach to evaluating

implementation dates for the conservation effort.

Response 24: We agree with the commenter's suggested change. Evaluation Criterion A.8. (formerly A.7.) now reads as: "An implementation schedule (including incremental completion dates) for the conservation effort is provided."

Issue 25: Commenters suggested that Criterion A.8. (now A.9.) be revised to read: "The conservation agreement or plan that includes the conservation effort include a commitment by the party(ies) to apply their legal authorities and available resources as provided in the agreement or plan."

Response 25: The participation of the parties through a written agreement or plan establishes each party's commitment to apply their authorities and resources to implementation of each conservation effort. Therefore, it is unnecessary to include the suggested language; criterion A.9. (formerly A.8.) remains unchanged.

Issue 26: A commenter also suggested adding a criterion: "Evidence that other conservation efforts have been implemented for sympatric species within the same ecosystem that may provide benefits to the subject species is provided."

Response 26: We do not think it is necessary to add such a criterion. At the time of listing, we will take into consideration all relevant information, including the effect of other conservation efforts for sympatric species on the status of the species we are considering for listing.

Issue 27: Several commenters recommended that we make specific changes to the Criterion B.1. language to read as: "The nature and extent of threats being addressed by the conservation effort are described, and how the conservation effort will reduce the threats are defined." In addition, commenters suggested we change Criterion B.2. to read as: "Explicit incremental objectives for the conservation effort and dates for achieving them should be stated."

Response 27: We agree that, in addition to identifying threats, the plan should explain how formalized conservation efforts reduce threats to the species. Therefore, Evaluation Criterion B.1. now reads as: "The nature and extent of threats being addressed by the conservation effort are described, and how the conservation effort reduces the threats is described." We agree that conservation efforts should include incremental objectives. This allows the parties to evaluate progress toward the overall goal of a conservation effort, which is essential for adaptive management. In addition, setting and achieving interim objectives is helpful in maintaining support for the effort. Therefore, Evaluation Criterion B.2. now reads as: "Explicit incremental objectives for the conservation effort and dates for achieving them are stated."

Issue 28: Some commenters recommended that the party's (ies') prior record with respect to development and implementation of conservation efforts be recognized towards their credibility and reliability to implement future conservation efforts. A commenter also suggested adding a criterion to read as: "Demonstrated ability of the party(ies) to develop and implement effective conservation efforts for this or other species and habitats." Another comment suggested that the history and momentum of a program should be taken into account (e.g., watershed council programs) when considering the certainty of effectiveness and implementation. These considerations would help ensure a high level of certainty that regulatory mechanisms, funding authorizations, and voluntary participation will be adopted by a specified date adequate to provide certainty of implementation.

Response 28: Although it would be beneficial for the party(ies) to demonstrate their past abilities to implement effective formalized conservation efforts for the focus species or other species and habitats, we do not believe that this is necessary to demonstrate a high level of certainty that the conservation effort will be implemented. In addition, a criterion that emphasizes previous experience in implementing conservation efforts may limit formalized conservation efforts to only those party(ies) that have a track record and would unjustifiably constrain consideration of efforts by those who do not satisfy this criterion. Such parties can provide certainty in other ways. We agree that a party's (ies') prior record and history with respect to implementation of conservation efforts should be recognized towards their credibility and reliability. Information concerning a party's experience in implementing conservation efforts may be useful in evaluating how their conservation effort satisfies the PECE criteria. The momentum of a project is a good indication of the progress that is being made towards a party's (ies') conservation efforts, but momentum can decrease, and thus cannot be solely relied upon to determine the certainty that a formalized conservation effort will be implemented or effective.

Issue 29: One commenter stated that our use of "must" in meeting the criteria is inappropriate in the context of a policy, and the policy should rather be treated as guidance.

Response 29: The only mandatory statements in the policy refer to findings that we must make. In order for us to find that a particular formalized conservation effort has improved the status of the species, we must be certain that the formalized conservation effort will be implemented and will be effective. No party is required to take any action under this policy. Rather the policy provides us guidance on how we will evaluate formalized conservation efforts that have yet to be implemented or have yet to demonstrate effectiveness at the time of our listing decision.

Legal Issues

Issue 30: Many commenters mentioned past litigation (i.e., decisions on coho salmon and Barton Springs salamander) in which the courts have ruled against the Services in cases that have involved Candidate Conservation Agreements or other conservation efforts, and question how the PECE policy addresses this issue. Commenters question how this policy will keep the Services from relying on speculative conservation efforts.

Response 30: We referenced past adverse decisions when we published the draft policy. The purpose of PECE, in part, is to address situations similar to those in which some courts found past conservation efforts insufficient. We developed the PECE to establish a set of consistent standards for evaluating certain formalized conservation efforts at the time of a listing decision and to ensure with a high level of certainty that formalized conservation efforts will be implemented and effective. We agree that we may not rely on speculative promises of future action when making listing decisions.

Issue 31: Several commenters questioned the legality of considering private party's (ies') input when section 4(b)(1)(A) of the Act states "* * * and after taking into account those efforts, if any, being made by any State or foreign nation, or any political subdivision of a State or foreign nation, to protect such species * * *" In addition, commenters stated that the PECE policy is inconsistent with the plain language and the congressional intent of the Act by allowing agencies to evaluate any private measures. They also stated that this was inconsistent with considering section 4(a)(1)(D), which only permits agencies to evaluate "existing regulatory mechanisms." They also stated that the

Services incorrectly conclude that section 4(a)(1)(E), "other natural or manmade factors affecting [the species'] continued existence," allows the Services to consider actions of "any other entity" in making listing determinations. One commenter stated that there are no provisions to authorize the Services to consider voluntary conservation agreements by other Federal agencies. In 1982, the Act omitted 1973 language for listing determinations made with "other interested Federal agencies." In addition, the commenters stated that the Act imposes conservation duties on all Federal agencies only after the Services have taken the initial step in listing the species.

Response 31: Please refer to the Policy Scope section for an explanation of our authority under section 4 of the Act to assess all threats affecting the species status as well as all efforts that reduce threats to the species.

Issue 32: One commenter suggested that we formalize this policy by codifying it in the Code of Federal Regulations. They suggest that by adopting this policy as agency regulation, we can make the policy more binding, provide a basis for judicial deference, and thus hopefully reduce the amount of litigation.

Response 32: We believe that codifying PECE in the Code of Federal Regulations is not necessary because it is intended as a policy to guide how we will evaluate formalized conservation efforts when making listing decisions.

Issue 33: Some commenters believe that all regulatory mechanisms must be in place prior to finalizing a conservation plan, while other commenters feel that this requirement may dissuade voluntary conservation efforts of private landowners. One commenter stated that, based on the amount of time usually needed to enact most regulatory mechanisms, it seems appropriate to set this minimum standard for evaluating formalized conservation efforts. This criterion should prompt more serious political consideration of adopting a regulatory mechanism sooner rather than later. Another commenter suggested that, instead of requiring regulations, we should require cooperators to identify and address any regulatory deficiencies affecting the species.

Response 33: In order for us to determine with a high level of certainty that a formalized conservation effort will be implemented, among other things, all regulatory mechanisms necessary to implement the effort must be in place at the time we make our listing decision. However, there may be situations where regulatory mechanisms are not necessary for implementing the conservation effort due to the nature of the action that removes threats, or there may be situations where necessary regulatory mechanisms are already in place.

Issue 34: One commenter stated that only when an alternative regulatory mechanism provides the same or higher protections than listing can the threat factors be said to be alleviated. A high level of certainty over future funding or voluntary participation might be acceptable if alternative regulatory mechanisms to prevent take in the interim are in place.

Response 34: Determinations to list species under the Act are based solely on whether or not they meet the definitions of threatened or endangered as specified by the Act. Through PECE, we will evaluate, at the time of our listing decision, whether a formalized conservation effort adequately reduces threats and improves the status of the species to make listing unnecessary. Additional alternative regulatory mechanisms to prevent take are not necessary if the threats to the species are reduced to the point that the species does not meet the definitions of threatened or endangered.

Issue 35: One commenter stated concern that the Services would not be able to provide assurances to private landowners because no specific provisions in the Act authorize conservation agreements in lieu of listing, and that third party lawsuits also undermine the Services' assurances. One commenter asked what future protection of their ongoing actions participants would receive.

Response 35: Satisfying the PECE criteria does not provide assurances that we will not decide to list a species. Also, because of the individual nature of species and the circumstances of their status, PECE does not address how much conservation is required to make listing unnecessary. Because of the numerous factors that affect a species' status, we may list a species despite the fact that one or more formalized conservation efforts have satisfied PECE. However, assurances can be provided to non-Federal entities through an approved Candidate Conservation Agreement with Assurances (CCAA) and in an associated enhancement of survival permit issued under section 10(a)(1)(A) of the Act. Many property owners desire certainty with regard to future regulatory restrictions to guarantee continuation of existing land or water uses or to assure allowance for future changes in land use. By facilitating this kind of individual land

use planning, assurances provided under the CCAA policy can substantially benefit many property owners. These agreements can have significance in our listing decisions, and we may also evaluate them according to the criteria in the PECE if they are not yet implemented or have not demonstrated results. However, we will make the determination of whether these CCAAs preclude or remove any need to list the covered species on a case-by-case basis in accordance with the listing criteria and procedures under section 4 of the Act.

Issue 36: Several commenters stated that the PECE does not always provide incentives to conserve species and is, therefore, not supported by the Congressional finding of section 2(a)(5) of the Act. The commenters stated that the parties lack incentives to develop conservation programs until after the species is listed (e.g., *Building Industry Association of Southern California* v. *Babbitt*, where listing the coastal California gnatcatcher encouraged enrollment in conservation programs.) In addition, they stated that PECE provides a means for the listing process to be avoided entirely, and, therefore, may often fail to provide incentives that Congress referred to in its findings in section 2(a)(5). They stated that the "system" of incentives to which that Congressional finding refers is already found in incidental take provisions in section 10 of the Act, which will better ensure development and implementation of successful conservation programs.

Response 36: PECE is not "a way to avoid listing" or an "in lieu of listing" policy. This policy outlines guidance on the criteria we will use to evaluate formalized conservation efforts in determining whether to list a species. Knowing how we will evaluate any unimplemented or unmeasured formalized conservation efforts may help parties draft more effective agreements. However, there is a conservation incentive because, if a species becomes listed, these efforts can contribute to recovery and eventual delisting or downlisting of the species. Also, see our response to Issue 35.

Issue 37: Several commenters stated that relying on unimplemented future conservation measures is inconsistent with the definitions of "threatened species" and "endangered species" as provided in section 3 of the Act, and that PECE's evaluation of future, unimplemented conservation efforts in listing determinations is inconsistent with both the plain language of the Act and Congressional intent. Also, the commenters stated that the PECE

erroneously claims that the definitions of "threatened species" and "endangered species" connote future status, not present status.

Response 37: We agree that, when we make a listing decision, we must determine the species' present status which includes, in part, an evaluation of current threats. However, deciding or determining whether a species meets the definition of threatened or endangered also requires us to make a prediction about the future persistence of a species. Central to this concept is a prediction of future conditions, including consideration of future negative effects of anticipated human actions. The language of the Act supports this approach. The definitions for both "endangered species" and "threatened species" connote future condition, which indicates that consideration of whether a species should be listed depends in part on identification and evaluation of future actions that will reduce or remove, as well as create or exacerbate, threats to the species. We cannot protect species without taking into account future threats to a species. The Act does not require that, and species conservation would be compromised if, we wait until a threat is actually impacting populations before we list the species as threatened or endangered. Similarly, the magnitude and/or imminence of a threat may be reduced as a result of future positive human actions. Common to the consideration of both the negative and positive effects of future human actions is a determination of the likelihood that the actions will occur and that their effects on the species will be realized. Therefore, we consider both future negative and future positive impacts when assessing the listing status of the species. The first factor in section 4(a)(1)—"the present or threatened destruction, modification, or curtailment of [the species'] habitat or range"—identifies how analysis of both current actions affecting a species' habitat or range and those actions that are sufficiently certain to occur in the future and affect a species' habitat or range are necessary to assess a species' status. However, future Federal, state, local, or private actions that affect a species are not limited to actions that will affect a species' habitat or range. Congress did not intend for us to consider future actions affecting a species' habitat or range, yet ignore future actions that will influence overutilization, disease, predation, regulatory mechanisms, or other natural or manmade factors. Therefore, we construe Congress' intent, as reflected by the language of the Act, to require us to consider both current actions that affect a species' status and sufficiently certain future actions—either positive or negative—that affect a species' status.

Issue 38: Several commenters stated that PECE's "sufficient certainty" standard is inconsistent with the Act's "best available science" standard. They stated that courts have ruled that any standard other than "best available science" violates the plain language and the Congressional intent of the Act. The commenters also stated that the "sufficient certainty" standard violates Congressional intent because it weakens the standard required by the Act to list species and can result in unnecessary, and potentially harmful, postponement of affirmative listing.

Response 38: We agree that our listing decisions must be based on the best available science. PECE does not address or change the listing criteria and procedures established under section 4 of the Act. Listing analyses include the evaluation of conservation efforts for the species under consideration. PECE is designed to help ensure a consistent and rigorous review of formalized conservation efforts that have yet to be implemented or efforts that have been implemented but have not yet shown effectiveness by establishing a set of standards to evaluate the certainty of implementation and effectiveness of these efforts.

Issue 39: Several commenters stated that PECE reduces or eliminates public comment on proposed rules to list species and is in violation of the Administrative Procedure Act (APA). Further, they stated that PECE violates the APA by allowing submission of formalized conservation measures after the proposed rule is issued to list species as threatened or endangered. Receiving "conservation agreements or plans before the end of the comment period in order to be considered in final listing decision" encourages landowners to submit conservation agreements at the last minute to avoid public scrutiny, and the PECE process could be a potential delay tactic used by landowners to postpone the listing of species. They stated that the Courts agree that failure of the Services to make available to the public conservation agreements on which listing decisions are based violates the public comment provision of the APA.

Response 39: All listing decisions, including those involving formalized conservation agreements, will comply with the requirements of the APA and ESA. If we receive a formalized conservation agreement or plan during an open comment period and it presents

significant new information relevant to the listing decision, we would either extend or reopen the public comment period to solicit public comments specifically addressing that plan or agreement. We recognize, however, that there may be situations where APA requirements must be reconciled with the ESA's statutory deadlines.

Issue 40: Several commenters expressed their concern that conservation efforts do not have binding obligations.

Response 40: While PECE does not require participants to have binding obligations, the policy does require a high level of certainty that a conservation effort will be implemented and effective at the time we make our listing decision. Furthermore, any subsequent failure to satisfy one or more PECE criteria would constitute new information and, depending on the significance of the formalized conservation effort to the species' status, may require a reevaluation of whether there is an increased risk of extinction, and whether that increased risk indicates that the species' status is threatened or endangered.

Funding Issues

Issue 41: Several commenters requested that we further specify our criteria stating that "a high level of certainty that the party(ies) to the agreement or plan that will implement the conservation effort will obtain the necessary funding is provided." In addition, one commenter questioned whether "a high level of certainty" for authorizations or funding was really an improvement over the status quo and suggested that we either list the required elements we will use to evaluate completeness of the conservation efforts or quantitatively define an evaluation standard.

Response 41: A high level of certainty of funding does not mean that funding must be in place now for implementation of the entire plan, but rather, it means that we must have convincing information that funding will be provided each year to implement relevant conservation efforts. We believe that at least 1 year of funding should be assured, and we should have documentation that demonstrates a commitment to obtain future funding, e.g., documentation showing funding for the first year is in place and a written commitment from the senior official of a state agency or organization to request or provide necessary funding in subsequent budget cycles, or documentation showing that funds are available through appropriations to existing programs and the

implementation of this plan is a priority for these programs. A fiscal schedule or plan showing clear links to the implementation schedule should be provided, as well as an explanation of how the party(ies) will obtain future necessary funding. It is also beneficial for entities to demonstrate that similar funding was requested and obtained in the past since this funding history can show the likelihood that future funding will be obtained.

Issue 42: One commenter suggested that the PECE policy holds qualifying conservation efforts to a higher standard than recovery plans. The commenter quoted several existing recovery plans that included disclaimers about budget commitments associated with specific tasks. Therefore, the commenter concluded that it is unrealistic and unreasonable to mandate that funding be in place when a conservation effort is evaluated.

Response 42: The Act does not require that certainty of implementation be provided for recovery management actions for listed species or conservation efforts for nonlisted species. Likewise, the PECE does not require that certainty of implementation be provided for during development of conservation efforts for nonlisted species. It is inappropriate to consider the PECE as holding conservation plans or agreements to a higher standard than the standard that exists for recovery plans because the PECE does not mandate a standard for conservation plans or agreements at the time of plan development. Rather, the PECE provides us guidance for the evaluation of conservation efforts when making a listing decision for a nonlisted species.

Recovery plans for listed species and conservation plans or agreements for nonlisted species identify needed conservation actions but may or may not provide certainty that the actions will be implemented or effective. However, when making a listing decision for nonlisted species, we must consider the certainty that a conservation effort will be implemented and effective. The PECE establishes criteria for us to use in evaluating conservation efforts when making listing decisions.

It is possible that we would evaluate a management action identified in a recovery plan for a listed species using the PECE. If, for example, a yet-to-be-implemented task identified in a recovery plan for a listed species would also benefit a nonlisted species, we, in making a listing decision for the nonlisted species, would apply the PECE criteria to that task to determine whether it could be considered as contributing to a decision not to list the species or to list the species as threatened rather than endangered. In this situation, we would evaluate the management task identified in a recovery plan using the PECE criteria in the same way as other conservation efforts for the nonlisted species. That is, the recovery plan task would be held to the same evaluation standard in the listing decision as other conservation efforts.

Foreign Species Issues

Issue 43: One commenter asked why the proposed policy excluded conservation efforts by foreign governments, even though section 4(b)(1)(A) of the Act requires the Services to take such efforts into account. This commenter also stated that the proposed policy is contrary to "The Foreign Relations Law of the United States," which he argues requires the United States to defer to other nations when they have a "clearly greater interest" regarding policies or regulations being considered by the United States that could negatively affect their nations.

Response 43: As required by the Act, we have taken and will continue to take into account conservation efforts by foreign countries when considering listing of foreign species (sections 4(b) and 8 of the Act). Furthermore, whenever a species whose range occurs at least in part outside of the United States is proposed for a listing action (listing, change in status, or delisting), we communicate with and solicit the input of the countries within the range of the species. At that time, countries are provided the opportunity to share information on the status of the species, management of the species, and on conservation efforts within the foreign country. We will take those comments and information provided into consideration when evaluating the listing action, which by law must follow the analysis outlined in sections 4(a) and 4(b) of the Act. Thus, all listing decisions for foreign species will continue to comply with the provisions of the Act.

Issues Outside Scope of Policy

We received several comments that were outside of the scope of PECE. Below, we have briefly addressed these comments.

Issue 44: A comment was made that the Services should not list foreign species under the Act when such listing is in conflict with the Convention on International Trade in Endangered Species of Wild Fauna and Flora (CITES).

Response 44: Considerations regarding CITES are outside the scope of the PECE. However, we do not believe there is a conflict with CITES and listing of a foreign species under the Act. When evaluating the status of foreign species under the Act, we take into consideration whether the species is listed under CITES (and if listed, at what level) and all available information regarding the listing. If you have questions regarding CITES, please contact the FWS Division of Scientific Authority at 4401 N. Fairfax Drive, Room 750, Arlington, VA 22203 or by telephone at 703–358–1708.

Issue 45: One commenter stated that all conservation agreements/plans should be subject to independent scientific peer review. This commenter also argued that any conservation agreement or plan for a candidate species should remove all known major threats for the species and convey a reasonably high certainty that the agreement or plan will result in full conservation of the species.

Response 45: We believe that scientific review can help ensure that formalized conservation efforts are comprehensive and effective, and we expect that most or all participants will seek scientific review, but we will not require a formal independent peer review of conservation plans at the time of development. If a formalized conservation plan is presented for a species that has been proposed for listing, all relevant information, including formalized conservation efforts, will be subject to independent scientific review consistent with our policy on peer review (59 FR 34270). We will also solicit public comments on our listing proposals.

The amount or level of conservation proposed in a conservation plan (e.g., removal of all versus some of the major threats) is outside the scope of PECE. Assuming that all of the PECE criteria have been satisfied for the efforts to which they apply, it stands to reason that plans that comprehensively address threats are likely to be more influential in listing decisions than plans that do not thoroughly address the conservation of the species. We believe that by establishing the PECE criteria for certainty of implementation and effectiveness, we are promoting the development of plans that improve the status of species. We expect that in some cases this improvement will reduce the risk of extinction sufficiently to make listing under the Act unnecessary, to result in listing a species as threatened rather than endangered, or to make classifying a

species as a candidate for listing unnecessary.

Issue 46: Several commenters questioned the extent of state involvement in the development of conservation efforts. One commenter said that the policy should mandate that States be involved with plan development, and that states approve all conservation efforts.

Response 46: It is outside the scope of PECE to establish standards to determine who participates in the development of conservation efforts and at what level. In many cases, states play a crucial role in the conservation of species. For formalized conservation efforts to be effective, it is logical for the states to play an integral role. To that end, we highly encourage state participation to help ensure the conservation of the species, but we do not believe that states should be mandated to participate in the development of all conservation plans. In some cases, states may not have the resources to participate in these plans, and in other situations, individuals or non-state entities may have the ability to develop an effective and well-implemented plan that does not require state participation, but that contributes to the conservation of a species. Through our listing process, we will work with state conservation agencies, and, if the listing decision involves a public comment period, states have a formal opportunity to comment on any conservation efforts being considered in the listing decision.

Issue 47: Several comments were made regarding the feedback mechanisms to correct a party's (ies') inadequate or ineffective implementation of a conservation effort. It was suggested that the Services specify clearly, and based on scientific information, those factors which the Services believe indicate that a conservation effort is either not being implemented or not being effective. Comments also suggested that party(ies) be given reasonable time (e.g., 90–120 days) to respond to the Service's findings by either implementing actions, achieving objectives, or providing information to respond to the Services.

Response 47: PECE is not a regulatory approval process, and establishing a formal feedback mechanism between the Services and participants is not within the scope of PECE. The final determination whether to list a species under the Act will rest solely upon whether or not the species under consideration meets the definition of threatened or endangered as specified by the Act, which will include consideration of whether formalized conservation efforts that meet PECE criteria have enhanced the status of the species. We will provide guidance to improve conservation efforts when possible, but we cannot delay listing decisions in order to participate in a corrective review process when the best scientific and commercial data indicate that a species meets the definition of threatened or endangered.

Issue 48: One commenter requested that we clarify how significant the conservation agreement must be to the species, and describe the anticipated overall impact/importance to the species and the estimated extent of the species' overall range that the habitat conservation agreement might cover.

Response 48: PECE does not establish standards for how much or what kind of conservation is required to make listing a species under the Act unnecessary. We believe that high-quality formalized conservation efforts should explain in detail the impact and significance of the effort on the target species. However, at the time of our listing decision, we will evaluate formalized conservation efforts using PECE to determine whether the effort provides certainty of implementation and effectiveness and improves the status of the species. Through our listing process, we will determine whether or not a species meets the definition of threatened or endangered.

Issue 49: Several commenters wrote that states do not have additional resources to be pro-active on candidate conservation efforts, and suggested that funding for conservation plans or efforts should be provided by the Federal Government.

Response 49: This comment is outside the scope of the PECE. This policy establishes a set of standards for evaluating formalized conservation efforts in our listing decisions and does not address funding sources to develop and implement these efforts.

Summary of Changes From the Proposed Policy

We have slightly revised some of the evaluation criteria as written in the proposed policy. We made the following changes to reflect comments that we received during the public comment period. We added the word "legal" to criterion A.2., incorporated additional language ("the commitment to proceed with the conservation effort is described."), and separated this criterion into two criteria (A.2. and A.3.). We revised criterion A.3. (formerly part of A.2.) to recognize that parties cannot commit to completing some legal procedural requirements (e.g. National Environmental Policy Act)

since some procedural requirements preclude commitment to a proposed action before the procedures are actually completed. We changed criterion A.5. (formerly A.4.) by adding "type" and "(e.g., number of landowners allowing entry to their land, or number of participants agreeing to change timber management practices and acreage involved)" and by replacing "why" with "how" and "are expected to" with "will." We deleted the word "all" at the beginning of criterion A.6. as we felt it was redundant. We added "(including incremental completion dates)" to criterion A.8. (formerly A.7.). To criterion B.1. we added "and how the conservation effort reduces the threats is described."

Also in the proposed policy we stated that if we make a decision not to list a species, or to list the species as threatened rather than endangered, based in part on the contributions of a formalized conservation effort, we will monitor the status of the species. We have clarified this in the final policy to state that we will monitor the status of the effort, including the progress of implementation of the formalized conservation effort.

Required Determinations

Regulatory Planning and Review

In accordance with Executive Order 12866, this document is a significant policy and was reviewed by the Office of Management and Budget (OMB) in accordance with the four criteria discussed below.

(a) This policy will not have an annual economic effect of $100 million or more or adversely affect an economic sector, productivity, jobs, the environment, or other units of government. The policy for the evaluation of conservation efforts when making listing decisions does not pertain to commercial products or activities or anything traded in the marketplace.

(b) This policy is not expected to create inconsistencies with other agencies' actions. FWS and NMFS are responsible for carrying out the Act.

(c) This policy is not expected to significantly affect entitlements, grants, user fees, loan programs, or the rights and obligations of their recipients.

(d) OMB has determined that this policy may raise novel legal or policy issues and, as a result, this action has undergone OMB review.

Regulatory Flexibility Act (5 U.S.C. 601 et seq.)

Under the Regulatory Flexibility Act (5 U.S.C. 601 *et seq.*, as amended by the

Small Business Regulatory Enforcement Fairness Act (SBREFA) of 1996), whenever an agency is required to publish a notice of rulemaking for any proposed or final rule, it must prepare and make available for public comment a regulatory flexibility analysis that describes the effect of the rule on small entities (i.e., small businesses, small organizations, and small government jurisdictions), unless the agency certifies that the rule will not have a significant economic impact on a substantial number of small entities.

SBREFA amended the Regulatory Flexibility Act to require Federal agencies to provide the statement of the factual basis for certifying that a rule will not have a significant economic impact on a substantial number of small entities. The following discussion explains our determination.

We have examined this policy's potential effects on small entities as required by the Regulatory Flexibility Act and have determined that this action will not have a significant economic impact on a substantial number of small entities since the policy will not result in any significant additional expenditures by entities that develop formalized conservation efforts. The criteria in this policy describe how we will evaluate elements that are already included in conservation efforts and do not establish any new implementation burdens. Therefore, we believe that no economic effects on States and other entities will result from compliance with the criteria in this policy.

Pursuant to the Regulatory Flexibility Act, at the proposed policy stage, we certified to the Small Business Administration that this policy would not have a significant economic impact on a substantial number of small entities, since we expect that this policy will not result in any significant additional expenditures by entities that develop formalized conservation efforts. We received no comments regarding the economic impacts of this policy on small entities. Thus, we certify that this final policy will not have a significant adverse impact on a substantial number of small entities and conclude that a regulatory flexibility analysis is not necessary.

We have determined that this policy will not cause (a) any effect on the economy of $100 million or more, (b) any increases in costs or prices for consumers; individual industries; Federal, State, or local government agencies; or geographical regions, or (c) any significant adverse effects on competition, employment, investment, productivity, innovation, or the ability of U.S.-based enterprises to compete with foreign-based enterprises (see Economic Analysis below).

Executive Order 13211

On May 18, 2001, the President issued an Executive Order (E.O. 13211) on regulations that significantly affect energy supply, distribution, and use. Executive Order 13211 requires agencies to prepare Statements of Energy Effects when undertaking certain actions. Although this policy is a significant action under Executive Order 12866, it is not expected to significantly affect energy supplies, distribution, or use. Therefore, this action is not a significant energy action and no Statement of Energy Effects is required.

Unfunded Mandates Reform Act (2 U.S.C. 1501 et seq.)

In accordance with the Unfunded Mandates Reform Act (2 U.S.C. 1501 *et seq.*):

(a) This policy will not "significantly or uniquely" affect small governments. A Small Government Agency Plan is not required. We expect that this policy will not result in any significant additional expenditures by entities that develop formalized conservation efforts.

(b) This policy will not produce a Federal mandate on state, local, or tribal governments or the private sector of $100 million or greater in any year; that is, it is not a "significant regulatory action" under the Unfunded Mandates Reform Act. This policy imposes no obligations on state, local, or tribal governments (see Economic Analysis below).

Takings

In accordance with Executive Order 12630, this policy does not have significant takings implications. While state, local or Tribal governments, or private entities may choose to directly or indirectly implement actions that may have property implications, they would do so as a result of their own decisions, not as a result of this policy. This policy has no provision that would take private property.

Federalism

In accordance with Executive Order 13132, this policy does not have significant Federalism effects. A Federalism assessment is not required. In keeping with Department of the Interior and Commerce policy, we requested information from and coordinated development of this policy with appropriate resource agencies throughout the United States.

Civil Justice Reform

In accordance with Executive Order 12988, this policy does not unduly burden the judicial system and meets the requirements of sections 3(a) and 3(b)(2) of the Order. With the guidance provided in the policy, requirements under section 4 of the Endangered Species Act will be clarified to entities that voluntarily develop formalized conservation efforts.

Paperwork Reduction Act of 1995 (44 U.S.C. 3501 et seq.)

This policy contains collection-of-information requirements subject to the Paperwork Reduction Act (PRA) and which have been approved by Office of Management and Budget (OMB). The FWS has OMB approval for the collection under OMB Control Number 1018–0119, which expires on December 31, 2005. The NMFS has OMB approval for the collection under OMB Control Number 0648–0466, which expires on December 31, 2005. We may not conduct or sponsor, and a person is not required to respond to, a collection of information unless it displays a currently valid OMB control number. Public reporting burden for FWS collections of information is estimated to average 2,500 hours for developing one agreement with the intent to preclude a listing, 320 hours for annual monitoring under one agreement, and 80 hours for one annual report. The FWS expects that six agreements with the intent of making listing unnecessary will be developed in one year and that four of these will be successful in making listing unnecessary, and therefore, the entities who develop these four agreements will carry through with their monitoring and reporting commitments. Public reporting burden for NMFS collections of information is estimated to average 2,500 hours for developing one agreement with the intent to preclude a listing, 320 hours for annual monitoring under one agreement, and 80 hours for one annual report. The NMFS expects that two agreements with the intent of making listing unnecessary will be developed in one year and that one of these will be successful in making listing unnecessary, and therefore, the entities who develop this agreement will carry through with their monitoring and reporting commitments. These estimates include the time for reviewing instructions, searching existing data sources, gathering and maintaining the data needed, and completing and reviewing the collection of information. Send comments regarding this burden estimate, or any other aspect of this data

collection, including suggestions for reducing the burden, to the FWS and NMFS (see **ADDRESSES** section of this policy).

National Environmental Policy Act

We have analyzed this policy in accordance with the criteria of the National Environmental Policy Act (NEPA), the Department of the Interior Manual (318 DM 2.2(g) and 6.3(D)), and National Oceanic and Atmospheric Administration (NOAA) Administrative Order 216–6. This policy does not constitute a major Federal action significantly affecting the quality of the human environment. The FWS has determined that the issuance of the policy is categorically excluded under the Department of the Interior's NEPA procedures in 516 DM 2, Appendix 1 (1.10) and 516 DM 6, Appendix 1. NOAA has determined that the issuance of this policy qualifies for a categorical exclusion as defined by NOAA Administrative Order 216–6, Environmental Review Procedure.

ESA Section 7 Consultation

We have determined that issuance of this policy will not affect species listed as threatened or endangered under the Endangered Species Act, and, therefore, a section 7 consultation on this policy is not required.

Government-to-Government Relationship With Tribes

In accordance with the President's memorandum of April 29, 1994, "Government-to-Government Relations with Native American Tribal Governments" (59 FR 22951), E.O. 13175, and the Department of Interior's 512 DM 2, this policy does not directly affect Tribal resources. The policy may have an indirect effect on Native American Tribes as the policy may influence the type and content of conservation plans and efforts implemented by Tribes, or other entities. The extent of this indirect effect will be determined on a case-by-case basis during our evaluation of individual formalized conservation efforts when we make a listing decision. Under Secretarial Order 3206, we will, at a minimum, share with the entity that developed the formalized conservation effort any information provided by the Tribes, through the public comment period for the listing decision or formal submissions. During the development of conservation plans, we can encourage the incorporation of conservation efforts that will restore or enhance Tribal trust resources. After consultation with the Tribes and the entity that developed the formalized conservation effort and after careful consideration of the Tribe's concerns, we must clearly state the rationale for the recommended final listing decision and explain how the decision relates to our trust responsibility. Accordingly:

(a) We have not yet consulted with the affected Tribe(s). We will address this requirement when we evaluate formalized conservation efforts that have yet to be implemented or have recently been implemented and have yet to show effectiveness at the time we make a listing decision.

(b) We have not yet worked with Tribes on a government-to-government basis. We will address this requirement when we evaluate formalized conservation efforts that have yet to be implemented or have recently been implemented but have yet to show effectiveness at the time we make a listing decision.

(c) We will consider Tribal views in individual evaluations of formalized conservation efforts.

(d) We have not yet consulted with the appropriate bureaus and offices of the Department about the identified effects of this policy on Tribes. This requirement will be addressed with individual evaluations of formalized conservation efforts.

Information Quality

In Accordance with section 515 of the Treasury and General Government Appropriations Act for Fiscal Year 2001 (Public Law 106–554), OMB directed Federal agencies to issue and implement guidelines to ensure and maximize the quality, objectivity, utility, and integrity of Government information disseminated to the public (67 FR 8452). Under our Information Quality guidelines, if we use a conservation plan or agreement as part of our decision to either list or not list a species under the Act, the plan or agreement is considered to be disseminated by us and these guidelines apply to the plan or agreement. The criteria outlined in this policy are consistent with OMB, Department of Commerce, NOAA, and Department of the Interior. FWS information quality guidelines. The Department of the Interior's guidelines can be found at *http://www.doi.gov/ocio/guidelines/515Guides.pdf*, and the FWS's guidelines can be found at *http://irm.fws.gov/infoguidelines/*. The Department of Commerce's guidelines can be found at *http://www.osec.doc.gov/cio/oipr/iqg.html*, and the NOAA/NMFS's guidelines can be found at *http://www.noaanews.noaa.gov/stories/iq.htm*. Under these guidelines, any affected

person or organization may request from FWS or NMFS, a correction of information they believe to be incorrect in the plan or agreement. "Affected persons or organizations" are those who may use, be benefitted by, or be harmed by the disseminated information (i.e., the conservation plan or agreement). The process for submitting a request for correction of information is found in the respective FWS and NOAA guidelines.

Economic Analysis

This policy identifies criteria that a formalized conservation effort must satisfy to ensure certainty of implementation and effectiveness and for us to determine that the conservation effort contributes to making listing a species unnecessary or contributes to forming a basis for listing a species as threatened rather than endangered. We developed this policy to ensure consistent and adequate evaluation of agreements and plans when making listing decisions. The policy will also provide guidance to States and other entities on how we will evaluate certain formalized conservation efforts during the listing process.

The criteria in this policy primarily describe elements that are already included in conservation efforts and that constitute sound conservation planning. For example, the criteria requiring identification of responsible parties, obtaining required authorizations, establishment of objectives, and inclusion of an implementation schedule and monitoring provisions are essential for directing the implementation and affirming the effectiveness of conservation efforts. These kinds of "planning" requirements are generally already included in conservation efforts and do not establish any new implementation burdens. Rather, these requirements will help to ensure that conservation efforts are well planned and, therefore, increase the likelihood that conservation efforts will ultimately be successful in making listing species unnecessary.

The development of an agreement or plan by a state or other entity is completely voluntary. However, when a state or other entity voluntarily decides to develop an agreement or plan with the specific intent of making listing a species unnecessary, the criteria identified in this policy can be construed as requirements placed on the development of such agreements or plans. The state or other entity must satisfy these criteria in order to obtain and retain the benefit they are seeking, which is making listing of a species as threatened or endangered unnecessary.

The criteria in the policy require demonstrating certainty of implementation and effectiveness of formalized conservation efforts. We have always considered the certainty of implementation and effectiveness of conservation efforts when making listing decisions. Therefore, we believe that no economic effects on states and other entities will result from using the criteria in this policy as guidance.

Furthermore, publication of this policy will have positive effects by informing States and other entities of the criteria we will use in evaluating formalized conservation efforts when making listing decisions, and thereby guide states and other entities in developing voluntary formalized conservation efforts that will be successful in making listing unnecessary. Therefore, we believe that informational benefits will result from issuing this policy. We believe these benefits, although important, will be insignificant economically.

Authority

The authority for this action is the Endangered Species Act of 1973, as amended (16 U.S.C. 1531 *et seq.*).

Policy for Evaluation of Conservation Efforts When Making Listing Decisions

Policy Purpose

The Fish and Wildlife Service and National Marine Fisheries Service developed this policy to ensure consistent and adequate evaluation of formalized conservation efforts (conservation efforts identified in conservation agreements, conservation plans, management plans, and similar documents) when making listing decisions under the Act. This policy may also guide the development of conservation efforts that sufficiently improve a species' status so as to make listing the species as threatened or endangered unnecessary.

Definitions

"Adaptive management" is a method for examining alternative strategies for meeting measurable biological goals and objectives, and then, if necessary, adjusting future conservation management actions according to what is learned.

"Agreements and plans" include conservation agreements, conservation plans, management plans, or similar documents approved by Federal agencies, State and local governments, Tribal governments, businesses, organizations, or individuals.

"Candidate species," as defined by regulations at 50 CFR 424.02(b), means any species being considered for listing as an endangered or a threatened species, but not yet the subject of a proposed rule. However, the FWS includes as candidate species those species for which the FWS has sufficient information on file relative to status and threats to support issuance of proposed listing rules. The NMFS includes as candidate species those species for which it has information indicating that listing may be warranted, but for which sufficient information to support actual proposed listing rules may be lacking. The term "candidate species" used in this policy refers to those species designated as candidates by either of the Services.

"Conservation efforts," for the purpose of this policy, are specific actions, activities, or programs designed to eliminate or reduce threats or otherwise improve the status of a species. Conservation efforts may involve restoration, enhancement, maintenance, or protection of habitat; reduction of mortality or injury; or other beneficial actions.

"Formalized conservation efforts" are conservation efforts identified in a conservation agreement, conservation plan, management plan, or similar document. An agreement or plan may contain numerous conservation efforts.

Policy Scope

When making listing decisions, the Services will evaluate whether formalized conservation efforts contribute to making it unnecessary to list a species, or to list a species as threatened rather than endangered. This policy applies to those formalized conservation efforts that have not yet been implemented or have been implemented, but have not yet demonstrated whether they are effective at the time of a listing decision. We will make this evaluation based on the certainty of implementing the conservation effort and the certainty that the effort will be effective. This policy identifies the criteria we will use to help determine the certainty of implementation and effectiveness. Listing decisions covered by the policy include findings on petitions to list species, and decisions on whether to assign candidate status, remove candidate status, issue proposed listing rules, and finalize or withdraw proposed listing rules. This policy applies to formalized conservation efforts developed with or without a specific intent to influence a listing decision and with or without the involvement of the Services.

Section 4(a)(1) of the Endangered Species Act of 1973, as amended (16

U.S.C. 1533(a)(1)), states that we must determine whether a species is threatened or endangered because of any of the following five factors:(A) the present or threatened destruction, modification, or curtailment of its habitat or range; (B) overutilization for commercial, recreational, scientific, or educational purposes; (C) disease or predation; (D) the inadequacy of existing regulatory mechanisms; or (E) other natural or manmade factors affecting its continued existence.

Although this language focuses on impacts negatively affecting a species, section 4(b)(1)(A) requires us also to "tak[e] into account those efforts, if any, being made by any State or foreign nation, or any political subdivision of a State or foreign nation, to protect such species, whether by predator control, protection of habitat and food supply, or other conservation practices, within any area under its jurisdiction, or on the high seas." Read together, sections 4(a)(1) and 4(b)(1)(A), as reflected in our regulations at 50 CFR 424.11(f), require us to take into account any State or local laws, regulations, ordinances, programs, or other specific conservation measures that either positively or negatively affect a species' status (i.e., measures that create, exacerbate, reduce, or remove threats identified through the section 4(a)(1) analysis). The manner in which the section 4(a)(1) factors are framed supports this conclusion. Factor (D) for example—ldquo;the inadequacy of existing regulatory mechanisms"— indicates that overall we might find existing regulatory mechanisms adequate to justify a determination not to list a species.

Factor (E) in section 4(a)(1) (any "manmade factors affecting [the species'] continued existence") requires us to consider the pertinent laws, regulations, programs, and other specific actions of any entity that either positively or negatively affect the species. Thus, the analysis outlined in section 4 of the Act requires us to consider the conservation efforts of not only State and foreign governments but also of Federal agencies, Tribal governments, businesses, organizations, or individuals that positively affect the species' status.

While conservation efforts are often informal, such as when a property owner implements conservation measures for a species simply because of concern for the species or interest in protecting its habitat, and without any specific intent to affect a listing decision, conservation efforts are often formalized in conservation agreements, conservation plans, management plans, or similar documents. The development

and implementation of such agreements and plans has been an effective mechanism for conserving declining species and has, in some instances, made listing unnecessary. These efforts are consistent with the Act's finding that "encouraging the States and other interested parties * * * to develop and maintain conservation programs * * * is a key * * * to better safeguarding, for the benefit of all citizens, the Nation's heritage in fish, wildlife, and plants" (16 U.S.C. 1531 (a)(5)).

In some situations, a listing decision must be made before all formalized conservation efforts have been implemented or before an effort has demonstrated effectiveness. We may determine that a formalized conservation effort that has not yet been implemented has reduced or removed a threat to a species when we have sufficient certainty that the effort will be implemented and will be effective.

Determining whether a species meets the definition of threatened or endangered requires us to analyze a species' risk of extinction. Central to this risk analysis is an assessment of the status of the species (i.e., is it in decline or at risk of decline and at what rate is the decline or risk of decline) and consideration of the likelihood that current or future conditions or actions will promote (see section 4(b)(1)(A)) or threaten a species' persistence. This determination requires us to make a prediction about the future persistence of a species, including consideration of both future negative and positive effects of anticipated human actions. The language of the Act supports this approach. The definitions for both "endangered species" and "threatened species" connote future condition, which indicates that consideration of whether a species should be listed depends in part on identification and evaluation of future actions that will reduce or remove, as well as create or exacerbate, threats to the species. The first factor in section 4(a)(1)—"the present or *threatened* destruction, modification, or curtailment of [the species'] habitat or range"—identifies how analysis of both current actions affecting a species' habitat or range and those actions that are sufficiently certain to occur in the future and affect a species' habitat or range are necessary to assess a species' status. However, future Federal, State, local, or private actions that affect a species are not limited to actions that will affect a species' habitat or range. Congress did not intend for us to consider future actions affecting a species' habitat or range, yet ignore future actions that will influence overutilization, disease, predation, regulatory mechanisms, or other natural or manmade factors. Therefore, we construe Congress' intent, as reflected by the language of the Act, to require us to consider both current actions that affect a species' status and sufficiently certain future actions—either positive or negative—that affect a species' status. As part of our assessment of future conditions, we will determine whether a formalized conservation effort that has yet to be implemented or has recently been implemented but has yet to show effectiveness provides a high level of certainty that the effort will be implemented and/or effective and results in the elimination or adequate reduction of the threats.

For example, if a state recently designed and approved a program to eliminate collection of a reptile being considered for listing, we must assess how this program affects the status of the species. Since the program was just designed, an implementation and effectiveness record may not yet exist. Therefore, we must evaluate the likelihood, or certainty, that it will be implemented and effective, using evidence such as the State's ability to enforce new regulations, educate the public, monitor compliance, and monitor the effects of the program on the species. Consequently, we would determine that the program reduces the threat of overutilization of the species through collecting if we found sufficient certainty that the program would be implemented and effective.

In another example, a state could have a voluntary incentive program for protection and restoration of riparian habitat that includes providing technical and financial assistance for fencing to exclude livestock. Since the state has already implemented the program, the state does not need to provide certainty that it will be implemented. If the program was only recently implemented and no record of the effects of the program on the species' status existed, we would evaluate the effectiveness of this voluntary program at the time of our listing decision. To assess the effectiveness, we would evaluate the level of participation (e.g., number of participating landowners or number of stream-miles fenced), the length of time of the commitment by landowners, and whether the program reduces the threats on the species. We would determine that the program reduces the threat of habitat loss and degradation if we find sufficient certainty that the program is effective.

In addition, we will consider the estimated length of time that it will take for a formalized conservation effort to produce a positive effect on the species. In some cases, the nature, severity, and/or imminence of threats to a species may be such that a formalized conservation effort cannot be expected to produce results quickly enough to make listing unnecessary since we must determine at the time of the listing decision that the conservation effort has improved the status of the species.

Federal agencies, Tribal governments, state and local governments, businesses, organizations, or individuals contemplating development of an agreement or plan should be aware that, because the Act mandates specific timeframes for making listing decisions, we cannot delay the listing process to allow additional time to complete the development of an agreement or plan. Nevertheless, we encourage the development of agreements and plans even if they will not be completed prior to a final listing decision. Such an agreement or plan could serve as the foundation for a special rule under section 4(d) of the Act, which would establish only those prohibitions necessary and advisable for the conservation of a threatened species, or for a recovery plan, and could lead to earlier recovery and delisting.

This policy provides us guidance for evaluating the certainty of implementation and effectiveness of formalized conservation efforts. This policy is not intended to provide guidance for determining the specific level of conservation (e.g., number of populations or individuals) or the types of conservation efforts (e.g., habitat restoration, local regulatory mechanisms) specifically needed to make listing particular species unnecessary and does not provide guidance for determining when parties should enter into agreements. We do encourage early coordination in conservation measures to prevent the species from meeting the definition of endangered or threatened.

If we make a decision not to list a species or to list the species as threatened rather than endangered based in part on the contributions of a formalized conservation effort, we will track the status of the effort including the progress of implementation and effectiveness of the conservation effort. If any of the following occurs: (1) a failure to implement the conservation effort in accordance with the implementation schedule; (2) a failure to achieve objectives; (3) a failure to modify the conservation effort to adequately address an increase in the severity of a threat or to address other new information on threats; or (4) we receive any other new information indicating a possible change in the status of the species, then we will reevaluate the status of the species and consider whether initiating the listing process is necessary. Initiating the listing process may consist of designating the species as a candidate species and assigning a listing priority, issuing a proposed rule to list, issuing a proposed rule to reclassify, or issuing an emergency listing rule. In some cases, even if the parties fully implement all of the conservation efforts outlined in a particular agreement or plan, we may still need to list the species. For example, this may occur if conservation efforts only cover a portion of a species' range where the species needed to be conserved, or a particular threat to a species was not anticipated or addressed at all, or not adequately addressed, in the agreement or plan.

Evaluation Criteria

Conservation agreements, conservation plans, management plans, and similar documents generally identify numerous conservation efforts (i.e., actions, activities, or programs) to benefit the species. In determining whether a formalized conservation effort contributes to forming a basis for not listing a species, or for listing a species as threatened rather than endangered, we must evaluate whether the conservation effort improves the status of the species under the Act. Two factors are key in that evaluation: (1) for those efforts yet to be implemented, the certainty that the conservation effort will be implemented and (2) for those efforts that have not yet demonstrated effectiveness, the certainty that the conservation effort will be effective. Because the certainty of implementation and effectiveness of formalized conservation efforts may vary, we will evaluate each effort individually and use the following criteria to direct our analysis.

A. The certainty that the conservation effort will be implemented:

1. The conservation effort, the party(ies) to the agreement or plan that will implement the effort, and the staffing, funding level, funding source, and other resources necessary to implement the effort are identified. 2. The legal authority of the party(ies) to the agreement or plan to implement the formalized conservation effort, and the commitment to proceed with the conservation effort are described.3. The legal procedural requirements (e.g. environmental review) necessary to implement the effort are described, and information is provided indicating that fulfillment of these requirements does

not preclude commitment to the effort. 4. Authorizations (e.g., permits, landowner permission) necessary to implement the conservation effort are identified, and a high level of certainty is provided that the party(ies) to the agreement or plan that will implement the effort will obtain these authorizations. 5. The type and level of voluntary participation (e.g., number of landowners allowing entry to their land, or number of participants agreeing to change timber management practices and acreage involved) necessary to implement the conservation effort is identified, and a high level of certainty is provided that the party(ies) to the agreement or plan that will implement the conservation effort will obtain that level of voluntary participation (e.g., an explanation of how incentives to be provided will result in the necessary level of voluntary participation). 6. Regulatory mechanisms (e.g., laws, regulations, ordinances) necessary to implement the conservation effort are in place. 7. A high level of certainty is provided that the party(ies) to the agreement or plan that will implement the conservation effort will obtain the necessary funding. 8. An implementation schedule (including incremental completion dates) for the conservation effort is provided. 9. The conservation agreement or plan that includes the conservation effort is approved by all parties to the agreement or plan.

B. The certainty that the conservation effort will be effective:

1. The nature and extent of threats being addressed by the conservation effort are described, and how the conservation effort reduces the threats is described. 2. Explicit incremental objectives for the conservation effort and dates for achieving them are stated. 3. The steps necessary to implement the conservation effort are identified in detail. 4. Quantifiable, scientifically valid parameters that will demonstrate achievement of objectives, and standards for these parameters by which progress will be measured, are identified. 5. Provisions for monitoring and reporting progress on implementation (based on compliance with the implementation schedule) and effectiveness (based on evaluation of quantifiable parameters) of the conservation effort are provided. 6. Principles of adaptive management are incorporated.

These criteria should not be considered comprehensive evaluation criteria. The certainty of implementation and effectiveness of a formalized conservation effort may also depend on species-specific, habitat-specific, location-specific, and effort-specific factors. We will consider all appropriate factors in evaluating formalized conservation efforts. The specific circumstances will also determine the amount of information necessary to satisfy these criteria.

To consider that a formalized conservation effort(s) contributes to forming a basis for not listing a species or listing a species as threatened rather than endangered, we must find that the conservation effort is sufficiently certain to be implemented and effective so as to have contributed to the elimination or adequate reduction of one or more threats to the species identified through the section 4(a)(1) analysis. The elimination or adequate reduction of section 4(a)(1) threats may lead to a determination that the species does not meet the definition of threatened or endangered, or is threatened rather than endangered. An agreement or plan may contain numerous conservation efforts, not all of which are sufficiently certain to be implemented and effective. Those conservation efforts that are not sufficiently certain to be implemented and effective cannot contribute to a determination that listing is unnecessary or a determination to list as threatened rather than endangered. Regardless of the adoption of a conservation agreement or plan, however, if the best available scientific and commercial data indicate that the species meets the definition of "endangered species" or "threatened species" on the day of the listing decision, then we must proceed with appropriate rule-making activity under section 4 of the Act.

Dated: September 16, 2002.

Steve Williams,

Director, Fish and Wildlife Service.

December 23, 2002.

William T. Hogarth,

Assistant Administrator for Fisheries, National Marine Fisheries Services.

[FR Doc. 03–7364 Filed 3–27–03; 8:45 am]

BILLING CODES 4310–55–S and 3510–22–S

DEPARTMENT OF COMMERCE

National Oceanic and Atmospheric Administration

50 CFR Part 679

[Docket No. 021212306–2306–01; I.D. 032403A]

Fisheries of the Exclusive Economic Zone Off Alaska; Pollock in Statistical Area 610 of the Gulf of Alaska

AGENCY: National Marine Fisheries Service (NMFS), National Oceanic and Atmospheric Administration (NOAA), Commerce.

ACTION: Modification of a closure.

SUMMARY: NMFS is reopening directed fishing for pollock in Statistical Area 610 of the Gulf of Alaska (GOA) for 24 hours. This action is necessary to fully use the B season allowance of the total allowable catch (TAC) of pollock specified for Statistical Area 610.

DATES: Effective 1200 hrs, Alaska local time (A.l.t.), March 26, 2003, through 1200 hrs, A.l.t., March 27, 2003.

FOR FURTHER INFORMATION CONTACT: Mary Furuness, 907–586–7228.

SUPPLEMENTARY INFORMATION: NMFS manages the groundfish fishery in the GOA exclusive economic zone according to the Fishery Management Plan for Groundfish of the Gulf of Alaska (FMP) prepared by the North Pacific Fishery Management Council under authority of the Magnuson-Stevens Fishery Conservation and Management Act. Regulations governing fishing by U.S. vessels in accordance with the FMP appear at subpart H of 50 CFR part 600 and 50 CFR part 679.

NMFS closed the B season directed fishery for pollock in Statistical Area 610 of the GOA under § 679.20(d)(1)(iii) on March 19, 2003 (68 FR 13857, March 21, 2003).

NMFS has determined that, approximately 986 mt of pollock remain in the B season directed fishing allowance. Therefore, in accordance with 679.25(a)(2)(i)(C) and (a)(2)(iii)(D), and to fully utilize the B season allowance of pollock TAC specified for Statistical Area 610, NMFS is terminating the previous closure and is reopening directed fishing for pollock in Statistical Area 610 of the GOA. In accordance with § 679.20(d)(1)(iii), the Regional Administrator finds that this directed fishing allowance will be reached after 24 hours. Consequently, NMFS is prohibiting directed fishing for pollock in Statistical Area 610 of the GOA effective 1200 hrs, A.l.t., March 27, 2003.